D0777960

BARRON'S BUSINESS LIBRARY

International Finance

J. Manville Harris, Jr., Ph.D.
Associate Professor of Finance
Clemson University

BARRON'S

General Editor for *Barron's Business Library* is George T. Friedlob, professor in the school of accountancy at Clemson University.

© Copyright 1992 by Barron's Educational Series, Inc.

All inquiries should be addressed to:
Barron's Educational Series, Inc.
250 Wireless Boulevard
Hauppauge, New York 11788

Library of Congress Catalog Card No. 91-36071

International Standard Book No. 0-8120-4812-1

Library of Congress Cataloging-in-Publication Data

Harris, J. Manville.
    International finance / J. Manville Harris, Jr.
        p.   cm.—(Barron's business library)
    Includes index.
    ISBN: 0-8120-4812-1
    1. International finance.   I. Title.   II. Series.
HG3881.H3234   1992
332'.042—dc20
                                                            91-36071
                                                            CIP

PRINTED IN ITALY
2345   9929   987654321

Contents

Scope and Importance

INTRODUCTION AND MAIN POINTS

In a modern economy, neither businesses nor individual investors can afford to be ignorant of the basic concepts of international finance. Changes in exchange rates and differences in national inflation and interest rates can affect the competitive position of businesses regardless of whether they are engaged in international operations.

For companies that are engaged in international business, national differences in banking, commercial laws, regulations, and political stability also complicate decision making. Today's investors must also understand the effects of, and interactions among, exchange rates, inflation rates, and interest rates if they wish to maximize their returns and minimize their risks. The study of international finance constitutes an essential component of a modern business education.

After studying the material in this chapter:

■ You will be able to distinguish the factors that complicate financial decision making in an international environment.

■ You will be aware of the impact of changes in exchange rates on a company's competitive position.

■ You will see the impact of exchange rate changes on financial rates of return.

■ You will understand the nature of international political and credit risks as they relate to financial decision making.

■ You will recognize the advantages to investors and business managers of understanding the fundamental principles and techniques of international finance.

BENEFITS OF UNDERSTANDING INTERNATIONAL FINANCE

Integration of the world economy is proceeding at an accelerating pace. National boundaries of even the largest countries no longer insulate business and investors from foreign competition or opportunities. The United States financial system now ranks second in size to that of Japan. With the adoption of an integrated market in 1992, the European Economic Community replaces the United States as the largest single market for goods and services.

Businesses and investors who fail to familiarize themselves with the fundamental concepts of international finance have little hope of competing effectively or achieving optimal performance. The following sections introduce some examples of the types of problems that require an understanding of the basic principles and techniques of international finance.

Multinational Companies

Consider a manager of a medium-sized American auto parts manufacturer who must decide whether to expand production capacity to meet growing demand in Eastern Europe. The capital budgeting committee of the board of directors has asked her to evaluate the feasibility of opening a manufacturing plant in Poland. Our manager would need to be familiar with most areas of international finance.

First, she would need to ascertain *political and credit risk factors* relevant to the investment. What are the relevant tax laws, and how might they change over the life of the investment? What is the potential for labor strife, riots, military intervention? Are there restrictions on imports and exports, and how likely are they to change? What are the relevant health, safety, and environmental regulations, and how are they likely to evolve? What are the commercial laws and customs associated with accounts payable and accounts receivable? What are the costs and the availability of banking services? Are there any foreign exchange restrictions, and are they likely to change in the future? After ascertaining the relevant risk factors, our manager would have to estimate both the cost of controlling these risks and any unavoidable losses.

Second, our hypothetical manager would have to analyze the potential exposure of the company to *currency risk*. What is the exchange rate for converting Polish currency into dollars? What are the exchange rates between Polish currency and the currencies of other European countries that the plant might export to? What are the forecasts for currency exchange rates in the future? What instruments and techniques are available for hedging these currency risks? Upon completing an assessment of these risk factors, our manager would then have to estimate the *costs of hedging*, along with a range of net present values in dollars for the investment.

Third, our manager would have to investigate *interest rates* and *inflation rates* in all relevant countries. In which countries should financing be obtained? How much debt and how much equity? What maturity is most appropriate? Should the company obtain a Eurocurrency loan? At what rate will operating costs increase? Will competitors' prices increase as rapidly? Having addressed these questions, the manager would also have to assess the likelihood and availability of refinancing both in the United States and abroad.

Clearly, multinational business is not for the fainthearted or the uneducated. Nevertheless, companies will always be eager to confront the costs and complexities of multinational business when the potential rewards exceed the expenses and risks. A knowledge of international finance is the key to controlling the risks and estimating the rewards and expenses.

Importers and Exporters

Let us suppose that our American auto parts manufacturer is in no position to consider a multinational expansion and is considering only the feasibility of exporting to Eastern Europe from expanded domestic capacity. Familiarity with international finance would still prove valuable.

When considering a domestic plant expansion for the purpose of exporting, management would need forecasts of future exchange rates between Eastern European and American currencies. Costs would be in dollars, while revenues from parts sold in Germany would be in deutsche marks. How many dollars could the deutsche mark revenues be converted into in the future? Can the risks of future exchange rate changes be controlled? At what rate will inflation increase costs in America? At what rate will inflation raise prices in Germany? Management would have to provide answers to these questions, along with plans for controlling these risks.

Dealing with Eastern European auto parts importers would introduce additional credit risks. Who would provide the trade credit financing for the importers? Should the trade credits be denominated in dollars or foreign currency? Who would retain title to goods prior to delivery and sale, and how could the risks of transoceanic shipment be handled? Should the exporter or the importer bear the risk associated with exchange rate changes that occur between the receipt of the order and the receipt of payment? Management would have to provide answers before a decision to expand capacity for export could be made.

It is easy to see how unfamiliarity with the complexities of international finance could cause many domestic businesses to forgo opportunities to export. However, the costs of ignoring export opportunities are growing. In 1960, international exports as a percent of total world domestic product were less than 10 percent. Today, exports constitute almost 20 percent of total world domestic product. Economies of scale available to exporters offer enormous incentives to learn the principles and techniques of international finance.

Foreign Competition
Although a decision to ignore the complexities of international finance may appeal to some businesses, few really have that option in the modern world economy. Let us suppose that our auto parts manufacturer chooses to avoid any international activity. While it is true that the company will then not have to worry about foreign political risk or international credit risk, management could still benefit from a knowledge of exchange rates and their relation to interest rates and inflation rates.

Nearly every business must be concerned with its competition. In today's economy, that includes foreign competition, both existing and potential. In the absence of foreign trade, competition between domestic manufacturers focuses primarily on product innovation, quality, distribution, and cost. Foreign competition introduces new risk factors, many of which are outside the control of individual firms.

Consider the effect of a 20 percent increase in the number of Japanese yen that can be exchanged for a dollar in the foreign exchange market. A Japanese car radio that formerly cost $120 in the United States can now be sold for only $100 without any noticeable revenue effect on the Japanese manufacturer, because the $100 can be exchanged for 20 percent more Japanese yen. From the perspective of the Japanese manufacturer, who is concerned only with revenues in yen, the increase in the currency exchange rate offsets the reduction in the price of the radio. However, the resulting competitive advantage of the Japanese manufacturer over the American manufacturer is very real. Even if the Japanese manufacturer were to forgo reducing dollar prices in America, the 20 percent increase in yen obtained for each car radio could finance additional competitive efforts aimed at improving quality, innovation, and distribution.

In addition to future exchange rate changes, our purely domestic auto parts manufacturer also must worry about the competitive impact of foreign interest rates and inflation rates. Do lower interest rates in Japan enable Japanese companies to finance investments in plant and equipment at a lower cost than would be incurred by an American company? Does a higher inflation rate in the United States increase manufacturing costs at a faster rate than in Japan? To what extent can manufacturers expect the competitive effects of changes in exchange rates, inflation rates, and interest rates to offset one another?

International Investors

Consider the plight of an ordinary investor who is considering an investment in our auto parts manufacturer. Can an investor adequately evaluate the future prospects of the business without a knowledge of international finance? Even investors who are not interested in stocks benefit from a working knowledge of international finance. U.S. financial markets are only one part of a much larger global financial system in the 1990s. What is the cost to investors of an inadequate knowledge of international finance? Interest rates, inflation rates, exchange rates, and business activity fluctuate and interact throughout the world economy.

Suppose a British investor observes that U.S. government bonds offer higher rates of return than equivalent British government bonds. He would like to obtain the higher rate of return in the United States. However, the American bonds are priced and pay interest in dollars, not British pounds. An investor in foreign bonds must determine the current exchange rate between American dollars and British pounds when the bonds are purchased and estimate future currency exchange rates when the interest is paid. Is the American investment superior? How much confidence in estimates of future exchange rates can an investor have? Are there techniques for hedging the currency risk?

Suppose an American investor believes that a Japanese computer maker is destined to rise to the top of the industry and would like to participate in the rewards. To what extent will future exchange rate changes affect dividends? Does the price of the stock vary with the value of the currency? Can these risks be hedged with currency futures or options?

Suppose a Canadian investor wants to invest in stocks but fears the effects of a future recession. Would an investment in European and American stocks diversify some of the risk? Would foreign investments increase the risk? Are there alternatives to purchasing foreign stocks directly?

WHAT IS INTERNATIONAL FINANCE?

The preceding sections demonstrate the need for understanding some of the concepts of international finance. In this section, we formally define and examine some of the different areas of international finance. We begin by defining finance.

Finance is the economics of time and uncertainty applied to decision making. Analysis of the effect of timing and uncertainty on the value of future costs and benefits enables businesses and investors to make rational economic choices concerning alternate courses of action. Finance covers many areas of specialization, including banking, investment analysis, and financial management.

International finance is the analysis of the economics of time and uncertainty applied to decision making in the context of many different countries. Sovereign nations each have their own currencies, business laws, and political systems.

These national differences introduce new risks into the financial decision making process for business and investors. _Currency risk_ refers to uncertainties that result from dealing with multiple currencies. Within the context of different systems of business law, _credit risk_ refers to uncertainties associated with the conduct of everyday business transactions. _Political risk_ describes the uncertainties that result from dealing with different and changing political systems. The following sections describe these three types of international risk in more detail.

Currency Risk

When precious metals such as gold or silver were used as currency, international finance was less complicated. Most international transactions could be carried out with a scale for measuring the weight of the precious metal. The introduction of paper currency ushered in more difficulties. Since each country had its own paper currency, individuals who received funds in a foreign currency had to exchange that currency for the paper currency of their own country.

Although most paper currencies promised convertibility into a specific weight of precious metal, the conversion often took considerable time and expense. In some cases, the promise of convertibility was broken. The resulting uncertainty about future ratios of exchange between currencies introduced _currency risk_ into financial transactions.

Currency risk also involves uncertainties about differences in interest rates and inflation rates among countries. The relationship between interest rates, inflation rates, and currency exchange rates is not surprising. *Interest rates* are measures of the costs and rewards of borrowing and lending currencies. Inflation rates measure changes in the intrinsic value of currencies over time.

Political and Credit Risk

When a nation's perception of what is in its own self-interest changes, its commercial, regulatory, and tax laws, even its system of government, can change. If such changes occur, investors and business can suffer unexpected losses. The legal doctrine of sovereign immunity prevents recovery in the courts of one country, losses that were incurred as a result of political action in another country. *Political risk* (sometimes called sovereign or country risk) refers to the uncertainties surrounding the possibility of losses that might result from changes in a sovereign country's commercial laws, regulations, or taxes.

International credit risk is similar to political risk in that it refers to uncertainties and potential business losses that result from differences in commercial law among nations. However, political and credit risk are different. Whereas political risk refers to uncertainties about potential changes in a nation's commercial laws, credit risk refers to uncertainties about the nature of the existing commercial laws.

For example, suppose an American company ships products to a Latin American retailer and specifies payment in 90 days. How does the exporter evaluate the creditworthiness of the importer, and what recourse is there in the event of default?

CHAPTER PERSPECTIVE

International finance is a relatively new science. Until recently, American business managers and students have been able to ignore much of the international economic environment. However, the rapid expansion and increasing integration of the world economy now requires that managers and investors have a working knowledge of international finance.

This chapter answered the questions, what is international finance and can managers and investors benefit from a working knowledge of it? We find that international finance consists of the economics of time and uncertainty applied to decision making in the context of a world economy comprising many separate nations. It includes analysis of the effects of, and interactions among, currency exchange rates, interest rates, and inflation rates, along with analysis of international credit and political risk.

The study of international finance provides insights and answers to questions that face a variety of business managers and investors. Whether or not a company is engaged in international trade, familiarity with the concepts, theories, and techniques of international finance can improve the effectiveness of business managers. One can understand why the accrediting agencies for university degree programs in business now require course work in international finance.

The following chapters present the most important concepts in international finance. The material is presented in a manner that enables an ordinary businessperson or investor to understand the concepts with a reasonable amount of effort. Emphasis is on improving your ability to make decisions.

Basic Exchange Rate Concepts

INTRODUCTION AND MAIN POINTS

Much of international finance involves currency risk. Currency risk results from uncertainty about future exchange rates. In this chapter, we explore three definitions of an exchange rate. These definitions are not mutually exclusive; all three constitute accurate explanations of what exchange rates are and how they can be used. A careful study of exchange rate definitions will make the following chapters much easier.

After studying the material in this chapter:

■ You will be able to define an exchange rate in a manner suitable to the context in which you are asked.

■ You will understand and be able to relate the different conventions for exchange rate quotation.

■ You will be able to convert any amount of one currency into the corresponding amount of any other currency.

■ You will be able to price goods and services in any currency that you choose.

■ You will understand the concept of a cross exchange rate and be able to use it to evaluate alternative methods of converting one currency into another.

RATIOS OF CURRENCY EXCHANGE

The simplest definition of an exchange rate is that it is a ratio of exchange between currencies. If you have 100 British pounds and the bank will exchange them for 160 U. S. dollars, then

$$(160 \text{ dollars})/(100 \text{ pounds}) = (1.60 \text{ dollars/pound})$$

and the exchange rate is quoted as 1.60 dollars per pound. Viewed in this way, the exchange rate is simply the amount of currency that you pay divided by the amount of foreign currency that you receive.

Algebraic Ratios

Exchange rates are simply the number of units of one currency per unit of another currency. This enables us to use them algebraically. For example, suppose we know that the exchange rate for the French franc is 0.19 dollars per franc. We are asked to determine the value in dollars of 200 francs. From elementary algebra we know that

$$(\text{francs}) \, (\text{dollars/franc}) = (\text{dollars})$$

since on the left side of the equation francs in the numerator cancels francs in the denominator, which leaves dollars in the numerator. In our example, francs equals 200 and dollars/franc equals 0.19, so we calculate

$$(200) \, (0.19) = (38)$$

and conclude that the value of 200 francs is \$38. The same procedure can be used to calculate the value in dollars of any amount of foreign currency when we know the exchange rate expressed as dollars per unit of foreign currency.

Direct Versus Indirect Quotation

In the previous examples, we assumed that the exchange rate is expressed as dollars per unit of foreign currency. In practice, we often cannot make that assumption. We could have calculated the ratio of exchange between the dollar and the pound as

$$(100 \text{ pounds})/(160 \text{ dollars}) = (0.625 \text{ pounds/dollar})$$

and expressed the exchange rate as 0.625 pounds per dollar. Both exchange rates are essentially equivalent because we can interpret exchange rates as algebraic ratios,

$$\frac{1}{(\text{pounds/dollar})} = (\text{dollars/pound})$$

and see that

$$\frac{1}{(0.625)} = (1.60)$$

The value of a pound expressed in dollars is simply the reciprocal of the value of the dollar expressed in pounds.

When banks in any country deal with each other, it is customary to quote exchange rates in terms of dollars, even to the extent that a German bank dealing in the interbank market in France would quote the value of the deutsche mark in dollars rather than francs. A quotation expressed as dollars per unit of foreign currency is referred to as the *U.S. equivalent* or *American terms,* whereas a quote expressed as foreign currency unit per dollar is referred to as *European terms.*

Outside the interbank market, dealers in foreign exchange generally use the direct method of quoting foreign exchange. A *direct quote* expresses the exchange rate in units of the currency of the country in which the customer resides. For example, in France the value of the deutsche mark would be quoted to customers as 3.20 francs per mark. In Tokyo, the value of the Italian lira would be quoted to travelers as 0.125 yen per lira. An *indirect quote* would be the reciprocal of this rate, or 8.00 lira per yen.

Indirect quotes are rarely used outside the U.S. and Great Britain. For example, Japanese yen would be quoted at 138 yen per dollar in New York and 258 yen per pound in London. In the U.S., all currencies except the British pound are quoted indirectly. The British pound would be quoted at 1.93 dollars per pound in both London and New York, which is a direct quote in New York and an indirect quote in London. If these conventions confuse you, don't worry. A calculator with a reciprocal key (1/X) can always provide you with the type of quote you prefer.

Pricing Foreign Goods and Services

Regardless of the type of exchange rate quote that is available, the ability to use exchange rates as algebraic ratios enables us to determine the value of foreign goods and services in terms of domestic currency. Consider the following scenario.

A marketing agent for an American producer of dairy products finds that she can receive 150 schillings for each case of evaporated milk that she agrees to ship to Vienna. She checks *The Wall Street Journal* and finds that the current value of the Austrian schilling is 0.09 dollars. In order to determine the potential value of such a sale, she recognizes that

$$(\text{schillings}) \, (\text{dollars/schilling}) = (\text{dollars})$$

and therefore calculates

$$(150) \, (0.09) = 13.50$$

She reports to the company's managers that exports of evaporated milk to Austria could generate revenues of $13.50 per case.

This export opportunity intrigues management, since they have been receiving as little as $12.00 per case for domestic sales. They ask her to explore the possibility of exports to other European countries. She checks on British and German exchange rates with her local bank and receives a direct quote on the pound of 1.60 dollars and an indirect quote on the deutsche mark of 1.80 marks per dollar. She then proceeds to determine the foreign currency prices in Germany and Britain that would provide a minimum revenue of $12.00 to her company. Noting that

$$(dollars) \ (marks/dollar) = (marks)$$

and calculating

$$(12.00) \ (1.80) = 21.60$$

she realizes that she must receive at least 21.60 marks per case of evaporated milk shipped to Germany if she is to obtain revenues equivalent to a domestic sale. For the British market she recognizes that

$$(dollars) \ \frac{1}{dollars/pound} = (pounds)$$

and calculates

$$(12.00) \ \frac{1}{1.60} = 7.50$$

which implies a minimum selling price of 7.50 pounds per case in Britain. All that remains is for her to ascertain the feasibility of sales at these prices.

As demonstrated by these examples, a clear understanding of *exchange rates*, defined simply as ratios of currency exchange, removes much of the uncertainty associated with analyzing the potential benefits of international operations. Exposure to more sophisticated definitions can provide additional benefits.

MARKET PRICES OF CURRENCIES

In the previous section, we began to think of exchange rates as the value of one currency in terms of another. When we think of the value of everyday items such as groceries, we think of their price. When you observe that the price of a muffin in a grocery store is \$0.35, you know that the exchange rate for muffins is 0.35 dollars per muffin. Likewise, currency exchange rates can be viewed as the prices of various currencies. In examples used so far, we have assumed that the price of a British pound was \$1.60 in America and that the price of a dollar in Germany was 1.80 marks.

There are many types of prices for goods in our domestic economy, such as retail prices, discount prices, regulated prices, and legal prices. In free and unregulated economies, we observe *market prices*. Supply and demand determine market prices for such things as baked muffins. As selling prices are reduced, customers demand more muffins. As selling prices are increased, bakers supply more muffins. If the selling price is too high, bakers supply more muffins than customers demand. Grocers start reducing the price to attract more customers, and the lower price causes bakers to start reducing the supply. If the selling price is too low, bakers supply fewer muffins than customers demand. The shortage of muffins allows bakers to raise their prices, which in turn reduces customer demand and raises the bakers' supply. In the absence of regulation, the price of muffins will either rise or fall until it reaches a point at which the supply of muffins is equal to the demand for them. This equilibrium exchange rate between dollars and muffins is the market price of muffins.

Currency exchange rates are also prices, but in many instances they are not market prices. An *official exchange rate* is one that is set by government decree. When the supply does not equal the demand for a currency at its official exchange rate, the currency is often traded illegally at a *black market exchange rate* within the country. An *offshore exchange rate* refers to the unofficial price of regulated currencies that are traded legally in countries outside the jurisdiction of the government that sets the official rate.

Since the early 1970s, the currencies of most of the major Western economic powers have been traded freely and allowed to float up and down according to the supply and demand for them in international markets. Hence, they are valued at what are commonly referred to as *floating exchange rates*.

Because trading is free and unregulated, floating exchange rates are market prices. In order to benefit from understanding that today's major currency exchange rates are market prices, we now take a closer look at the nature of supply and demand in the foreign exchange market.

Demand for Foreign Exchange

Why would individuals and businesses demand foreign currency? They cannot purchase domestic goods and services with it. However, if they want to purchase goods and services abroad, they must first exchange their currency for the currency of the country in which those goods and services are produced. The *foreign exchange market* refers to the institutions and arrangements for carrying out this exchange of currencies. Hence, demand for a particular country's currency on the foreign exchange market actually reflects demand by foreigners for that country's goods and services.

The demand for currency is more easily explained by an example. However, we must first simplify the economic arguments. In order to do so, pretend that the only trade that can take place between the United States and Japan is the export of American wheat to Japan and the import of Japanese Toyotas into the U.S. Once you understand the effects of this simplified type of trade on the foreign exchange market, the implications can be easily extended to more realistic circumstances.

Consider the demand for Japanese Toyotas in the U.S. Assume that Americans will purchase 200,000 Toyotas if they sell for $6,250, but only 100,000 Toyotas if they sell for $10,000. These two amounts constitute two points on the American demand curve for Toyotas, as shown in Figure 2-1. For a demand curve, the possible prices of a product are listed on the vertical axis and the corresponding quantity of the product demanded at each of those prices is listed on the horizontal axis. Each point on a demand curve gives the quantity of product desired for a particular price. In our example, the point for a price of $10,000 indicates a quantity of 100,000 Toyotas demanded. The curve slopes down because, as prices are reduced, customers buy more of the product.

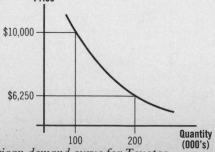

Fig. 2-1 *American demand curve for Toyotas*

Now consider the effect of this American demand for Toyotas on the foreign exchange market. American customers have dollars, but Japanese producers want yen. Therefore, Americans who want to buy Toyotas demand Japanese yen and supply American dollars in the foreign exchange market.

What would the demand curve for Japanese yen in the foreign exchange market look like? The horizontal axis is the quantity of yen demanded, and the vertical axis is the price of yen expressed as dollars/yen. For simplicity, assume that all of the demand for yen is the result of the American demand for Toyotas. Suppose the Japanese are willing to produce and export a Toyota for 1,250,000 yen. If the exchange rate is 0.008 dollars per yen, then the car can be sold in the U.S. for (1,250,000 * 0.008) = 10,000 dollars, which results in sales of 100,000 cars. Americans will demand (1,250,000 * 100 thousand) = 125 billion yen in the foreign exchange market. In Figure 2-2, we show a point on the demand curve that relates a price of 0.008 dollars per yen to a demand for 125 billion yen.

Let us now consider the effect of a reduction in the price of yen. Suppose we retain all of our previous assumptions but cause the price of yen to fall to 0.005 dollars per yen. The Japanese would still receive 1,250,000 yen per car if they sold them for (1,250,000 * 0.005) = 6250 dollars. However, Americans would now buy 200,000 Toyotas. This increased demand for lower priced Toyotas would result in an increased demand for yen in the foreign exchange market. The foreign exchange demand curve for yen in Figure 2-2 shows that a price of 0.005 dollars per yen corresponds to a demand for (1,250,000 * 200 thousand) = 250 billion yen.

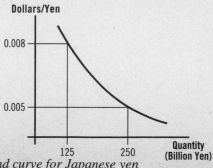

Fig. 2-2 *Demand curve for Japanese yen*

The downward slope of the demand curve for foreign exchange indicates that, as the price of a currency decreases, the demand for it in the foreign exchange market increases. The increased demand for the country's currency results from the desire of foreigners for more of the country's goods and services, since they now sell for a lower price in foreign countries. Although our example focused on autos, the effect of virtually all Japanese exports to America would be similar.

Supply of Foreign Exchange

The previous section explained what causes a demand for Japanese yen on the foreign exchange market. Why would the Japanese be willing to supply yen? Just as Americans would demand yen so that they could buy Japanese products, the Japanese would demand dollars in order to buy American products. Figure 2-3 shows the demand curve for wheat in Japan. At a price of 375 yen per bushel, the Japanese will purchase 20 million bushels but only 10 million bushels if the price is 600 yen per bushel.

Suppose American producers are willing to supply wheat for export to Japan at a price of $3.00 per bushel. The selling price of wheat in Japan will depend upon the exchange rate. At an exchange rate of 0.008 dollars per yen, wheat will sell for (3.00/0.008) = 375 yen per bushel. At an exchange rate of 0.005 dollars per yen, wheat will sell for (3.00/0.005) = 600 yen per dollar.

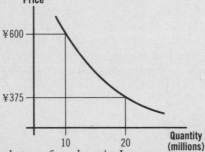

Fig. 2-3 *Demand curve for wheat in Japan*

If we assume for simplicity that trade in wheat constitutes the only transaction between the U.S. and Japan, then we can construct two points on the supply curve for yen in the foreign exchange market. Figure 2-4 shows that when the price of yen is 0.005 dollars, the quantity of yen supplied to the foreign exchange market is (600 * 10 million) = 6 billion yen. When the price of yen is 0.008 dollars, the supply of yen is (375 * 20 million) = 7.5 billion yen. The supply curve for yen slopes up, because at higher values for yen, the price of American goods and services in Japan is lower and the Japanese demand more of them.

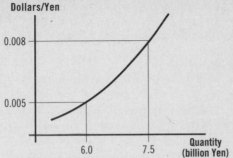

Fig. 2-4 *Supply curve for yen in the foreign exchange market*

Market Equilibrium

In the previous two sections, we have seen that the foreign exchange market for a currency such as the Japanese yen operates on the same principles as the market for commodities such as apples. The currency has an upward sloping supply curve, which means more is supplied at higher prices, and a downward sloping demand curve, which means that more is demanded at lower prices. Figure 2-5 shows the market for Japanese yen. As in any market, if the exchange rate is too high, the supply of yen will exceed the demand and its price in dollars will fall. Similarly, if the price is too low, the demand for the currency will exceed the supply and the exchange rate will rise. The *equilibrium* or *market price* of the currency is the exchange rate at which the supply of the currency on the foreign exchange market is equal to the demand for it.

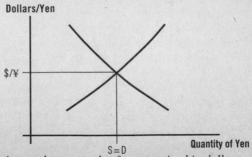

Fig. 2-5 *The foreign exchange market for yen priced in dollars*

Before moving on to the third and final definition of an exchange rate, let's examine the market price definition from another angle. In our example, we viewed the exchange rate as the price of the yen in dollars. We could have examined it from the perspective of its reciprocal, the price of the dollar in yen. Figure 2-6 shows the foreign exchange market for dollars priced in yen.

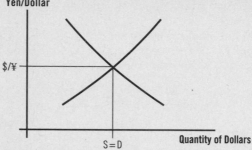

Fig. 2-6 *The foreign exchange market for dollars priced in yen*

Comparing this market to the market for yen shown in Figure 2-5, we see that the horizontal axis is now the quantity of dollars instead of yen and the price is now yen per dollar instead of dollars per yen. Both figures describe the same market.

Readers should think through the analysis of supply and demand in the market for dollars. It is helpful to remember that when the Japanese supply yen, they are also demanding dollars, and when Americans demand yen, they are also supplying dollars. We see that the factors that drive a currency exchange rate up drive the reciprocal of that exchange rate down.

INTERRELATED SETS OF PRICES
Up to this point, we have examined the exchange rate of a currency in terms of only one other currency. In practice, however, every currency has many exchange rates. The dollar can be valued in yen, but it also can be valued in pounds, marks, francs, lire, and any other currency. Although different, these various exchange rates for the dollar are interrelated, which provides the basis for our third definition. Exchange rates are sets of prices interrelated by triangular arbitrage.

Cross Rates
Before exploring triangular arbitrage, we must familiarize ourselves with the concept of cross rates of exchange. Suppose we

want to exchange American dollars for French francs. Our bank informs us that a dollar can be exchanged for 6 francs. We know that both dollars and francs can be exchanged for Italian lire. An alternative to exchanging dollars for francs directly is first to exchange dollars for lire and second to exchange the lire for francs. In either case, one begins with dollars and ends up with francs. We check with the bank and find that 1000 lire can be exchanged for a dollar and that one lira can be exchanged for 0.0062 francs.

From the first definition of exchange rates, we know that exchange rates can be manipulated as algebraic ratios. Using this concept, we can express the *cross rate* for the price of a dollar in francs as:

$$(\text{francs/lira}) \ (\text{lire/dollar}) = (\text{francs/dollar})$$

On the left side of the equation, lira in the denominator cancels lire in the numerator. Substituting the appropriate values of the lira, we calculate

$$(0.0062) \ (1000) = 6.2$$

and determine that the cross rate of exchange is 6.2 francs per dollar. Hence, we obtain more francs per dollar at the cross rate with the lira.

In our example, the cross rate of francs and dollars in terms of the lira is superior to the exchange rate for francs and dollars. However, we should still consider other cross rates for francs and dollars. Francs and dollars can both be exchanged for other currencies. There are as many cross rates as there are third currencies. We should explore all options. The procedure is the same. Compare the exchange rate for converting currency A into currency B with the cross rate obtained by first converting currency A into currency C and then converting currency C into currency B. Expressed algebraically,

$$(A/C) \ (C/B) = (A/B)$$

Cross rates for any two currencies (A/B) result from the algebraic cancellation of any third currency (C). In the event that you are quoted the exchange rate between currencies A and C as (C/A), simply use the reciprocal 1/(A/C).

The preceding discussion of cross rates ignores transactions costs. The cost of making currency transactions can introduce slight discrepancies between an exchange rate and its various cross rates. These issues are addressed in more detail in Chapter 3.

Triangular Arbitrage

Suppose you worked for a bank and observed that the exchange rate of the dollar was 6 francs at the same time that the cross rate was 6.2 francs. You could enrich your employer and advance your career by buying dollars for 6 francs, selling the dollars for 1000 lire per dollar, and then selling the lire for 0.0062 francs per lira. You would obtain a profit of 0.2 francs on every dollar. Transactions such as these are called *triangular arbitrage*.

The term arbitrage is used to describe the profitable practice of buying an item at one price and immediately selling it at a higher price. The wisdom of the arbitrageur is expressed in the well-known businesss rule "buy low and sell high." In our example of triangular arbitrage, we buy dollars for 6 francs and sell them for 6.2 francs. If the exchange rate had exceeded the cross rate we would have profited by buying at the cross rate and selling at the exchange rate. The arbitrage is triangular, since it involves three currencies.

Because arbitrageurs buy and sell currencies in their pursuit of profits, they create additional supplies of some currencies and additional demand for other currencies. This additional supply and demand has an effect on the market prices of the currencies.

Figure 2-7 shows the markets for the three currencies used in our example. The three vertical axes are labeled as the different currency prices used in our equation for the cross rate: francs per dollar, lire per dollar, and francs per lira. In each graph, the quantity corresponds to the currency in the denominator of each price. Since the arbitrageurs would buy dollars at a price of 6 francs, we show their effect as an increase in demand for dollars in the first graph by moving the demand curve to the right. The result is an increase in the market price of dollars in francs.

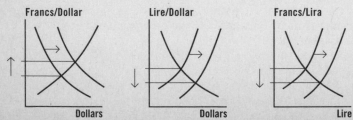

Fig. 2-7 *Markets for francs, lire, and dollars*

Since the arbitrageurs would exchange the dollars for lire at a price of 1000 lire per dollar, we show an increase in the supply of dollars in the second graph. The movement of the supply curve to the right lowers the lira price of dollars. The effect of the exchange of lire for francs appears as an increase in the supply of lire in the third graph, which lowers the price of lire in francs.

The combined effect of lowering the two prices that determine the cross rate of 6.2 francs per dollar, and raising the exchange rate of 6 francs per dollar reduces the arbitrageur's profit on any additional transactions. Competition among arbitrageurs keeps the profits from triangular arbitrage so small that a good rule of thumb in the foreign exchange markets is that cross rates are nearly equal to exchange rates.

Triangular arbitrage constitutes the mechanism by which the forces of supply and demand for a currency in one market are related to the forces of supply and demand for that currency in other markets. As a rule of thumb, we need only recall that a country's exports create a demand for its currency, while imports create a supply of its currency. The identity of the country to which the exports go, or the identity of the country from which the imports come, is of little importance. Triangular arbitrage spreads the effects to all markets. The net effect is that exports raise the value of a currency in terms of all other currencies, while imports reduce its value.

CHAPTER PERSPECTIVE

This chapter presents three definitions of an exchange rate. First, exchange rates are simply ratios of exchange between currencies. Second, exchange rates are the market prices of one currency denominated in another currency. Third, exchange rates are sets of prices interrelated by triangular arbitrage.

These definitions are not mutually exclusive, and knowledge of all three provides business managers and investors with insights that can improve their effectiveness. A thorough understanding of these definitions facilitates comprehension of most of the risks and rewards associated with international financial management.

Currency Exchange: Spot, Forward, and Futures Markets

3

INTRODUCTION AND MAIN POINTS

In this chapter, we explore some of the more important details of contractual arrangements for exchanging currencies. First, we examine the difference between the price at which we can buy a foreign currency and the price at which we can sell it. The factors that influence this difference, along with implications for businesses and investors, are discussed. Next, we distinguish between prices for currencies exchanged today and exchanges that take place in the future. The chapter concludes with an explanation of the nature and functions of currency futures markets.

After studying the material in this chapter:

■ You will understand the nature of bid/ask spreads and be able to anticipate differences in them.

■ You will comprehend the nature and implications of locational arbitrage and how it relates to bid/ask spreads.

■ You will understand the difference between spot and forward exchange rates.

■ You will recognize the advantages of being able to contract at forward exchange rates.

■ You will understand the difference between forward and futures contracts.

■ You will recognize the advantages and disadvantages of exchange rate futures contracts.

CURRENCY SPOT RATES

Because exchange rates vary over time, contracts to exchange currencies always specify the date on which the exchange takes place. Until recently, currencies could not be exchanged instantaneously; one had to allow a minimum of two business days for a currency transaction to take place. Today, most multinational banks offer their large corporate customers the option of same-day electronic conversion of currencies. The *spot exchange rate* refers to the price of currency that is exchanged immediately or as soon as possible. Such transactions comprise the *spot market*.

Bid and Offer Rates

In the previous chapter, we implicitly assumed that you can buy and sell foreign currencies at the same price. This assumption is common when analyzing the price of goods and services. However, consumers nearly always have to pay more for goods than they can sell them for.

The difference between the price at which goods can be bought and the price at which they can be sold provides the _operating margin_ that makes the business of retailing and wholesaling goods possible. The situation is no different for the business of exchanging foreign currencies. If we want to buy currency from a bank or dealer, we have to pay a higher price for it than we would receive if we sold that same currency to the bank or dealer.

A foreign exchange dealer's _bid_ rates are the prices that the dealer is willing to pay for foreign currencies. The _offer_ or _ask_ rates are the price at which the dealer is willing to sell the currency. For example, if a foreign exchange dealer at an international airport quotes a bid rate for deutsche marks of $0.54, then we can sell our deutsche marks to that dealer for $0.54 dollars per deutsche mark. If the dealer quotes an offer rate of $0.56 for deutsche marks, then we can buy deutsche marks from him for $0.56 dollars per deutsche mark.

The terms offer rate and ask rate or price are synonymous. Use of the term offer rate is widespread in the foreign exchange market, particularly in London. But its use can often confuse American readers, since the term offer can be interpreted as either an offer to buy or an offer to sell. Therefore, subsequent references to the price at which currency is offered for sale will use the term ask rate or price.

Bid/Ask Spreads

Because exchange rate dealers do not know beforehand whether a customer wants to buy or sell a currency, the bid and ask rates are typically quoted in pairs. For example, if a bank quotes the British pound at $1.8810—45, it has indicated its willingness to buy pounds for $1.8810 and sell them for $1.8845. You do not need to know whether by convention the bid price is quoted before the ask price or after. The higher price is always the ask rate, and the lower price is always the bid rate. If this were not true, any customer could bankrupt the dealer by simply engaging in an endless round of buying and selling the same currency.

We observe an apparent exception to the rule that ask rates exceed bid rates when exchange rates are quoted indirectly, as is true in the United States for currencies other than the pound. One can observe that an indirectly quoted bid rate for the Japanese yen, such as 125 yen per dollar, will always exceed the indirectly quoted ask rate, such as 120 yen per dollar. Yet this apparent exception to the rule is only an illusion, since indirect quotes are reciprocals of direct quotes. When the yen is quoted directly, the ask rate of $(1/120) = 0.0083$ dollars per yen exceeds the bid rate of $(1/125) = 0.0080$ dollars per yen.

The *spread* is the percentage difference between bid and ask quotes for foreign exchange:

$$\{(\text{Ask Price}) - (\text{Bid Price})\}/(\text{Ask Price}) = (\text{Spread})$$

For example, if the French franc is quoted $0.1950—85, the spread is calculated as

$$\{(0.1985) - (0.1950)\}/(0.1985) = 0.0176$$

or 1.76 percent. The spread can be viewed as the discount rate that foreign exchange dealers pay for currency that they then offer for sale. The spread also constitutes the percentage transaction cost to the customer for converting currencies.

Determinants of the Spread

Spreads vary widely, not only among different currencies but also among different dealers in the same currency. The size of the spread depends on both the degree of competition among dealers and the costs and risks borne by the dealer. A large spread is usually equally disadvantageous to buyers and sellers of a foreign currency, because it results from an ask rate that is higher and a bid rate that is lower than the rates on a quote that features a smaller spread. It is very unusual for a dealer to quote a favorable bid rate and an unfavorable ask rate, or vice versa. The dealer would attract more customers wanting to transact at the favorable rate than customers wanting to exchange currency at the unfavorable rate. Such practice would soon result in an imbalance between buy and sell orders, causing the dealer to have to balance his or her inventory by either buying or selling from another dealer.

Although an unfavorable spread is sometimes unavoidable, a knowledge of why spreads differ can often suggest sources for more favorable quotes. Foreign exchange dealers, located in international hotels and airports, who primarily serve travelers, quote some of the largest spreads. In these situations, the dealer bears relatively high costs, low volumes, and high risks. The dealer's costs result from the need to maintain an inventory of many currencies in a variety of denominations. Each transaction involves an individual customer who wants to exchange small amounts of currency but needs immediate delivery. Because of the need to maintain an inventory of currencies, the dealer is subject to the risk that the market prices of currencies may change during the time between the purchase and the sale of the inventory. In addition, the dealer often has limited competition. Customers who exchange currency in hotel lobbies are frequently more interested in speed and convenience than in getting the best price.

The interbank market features the smallest spreads. In the *interbank market*, banks exchange large amounts of currencies electronically, so inventories are not necessary. A bank can sell currency that it does not own and replace the borrowed currency with a later purchase. This is known as *covering a short position*. Transactions are instantaneous and do not involve the physical movement of currency. Banks can change quotations frequently with no prior notice. In addition, because the amounts of currency involved in individual transactions are very large, sizable profits can be generated by small spreads; for example, a spread of only one-hundredth of a percent on $100 million is $10,000.

Locational arbitrage also plays a role in controlling the size of the spread in foreign exchange markets. Suppose a foreign exchange manager at a multinational corporation simultaneously observes a bank in London quoting a bid rate for the pound of $1.9360 and a bank in New York quoting an ask rate of $1.9310. He could buy one million pounds in New York for $1.9310 per pound and immediately sell them for $1.9360 per pound. His company earns a locational arbitrage profit of (1 million $*$ $0.0050) = $5000.

Businesses and banks can profit from locational arbitrage any time the bid price of a currency in one location exceeds the ask price in another location. But the demand of arbitrageurs for the currency at the lower ask price will cause its price to rise, while the arbitrageurs' supply of the currency at the higher bid price will cause its price to fall. Hence, locational arbitrage keeps ask prices in one location from falling much below bid prices in another location. When one does observe a bid rate that is significantly higher than an ask rate in another location, investigation usually reveals impediments to simultaneous exchange or transaction costs that rule out profits from locational arbitrage.

FORWARD RATE CONTRACTS

While spot transactions refer to the immediate exchange of two currencies between two parties, forward transactions refer to contracts that commit the two parties to exchange specified amounts of two currencies at a specified time in the future. The spot exchange rate is the ratio of exchange in a spot transaction, while the *forward exchange rate* is the ratio of exchange in a forward transaction. For reasons that will be analyzed later, spot rates can exceed or be below forward rates for the same currencies.

The forward exchange market reduces the uncertainty that results from fluctuations in exchange rates. Consider the plight of an American exporter of lumber. Suppose the business has just arranged the sale of a shipment of logs to Japan for 130 billion yen. If the contract calls for immediate payment, the exporter can convert the yen into dollars at the spot rate of exchange. But if the contract calls for payment in 90 days, the exporter cannot be certain of his dollar revenue from the sale, because in recent years the price of yen in dollars has increased and decreased by as much as 30 percent over periods of three months. Such risks could prevent many exporters from doing business. Fortunately, exporters can avoid this risk by simultaneously arranging a forward exchange contract with a bank for the sale of 130 billion yen in three months.

Banks will generally provide instant quotes for both spot exchange rates and several forward exchange rates between the dollar and major currencies. Typically, a bank will quote forward rates for transactions that are to take place one month, two months, three months, six months, and 12 months in the future. Most large banks are willing to arrange forward transactions in less popular currencies and at other times in the future. Some banks have arranged forward contracts as far in the future as seven years.

Banks and dealers sometimes quote forward exchange rates in terms of annual *premiums* or *discounts* from the spot rate. Suppose we observe a 30-day forward rate of $1.919 and a spot rate of $1.900 per pound. The percentage by which the forward rate exceeds the spot rate is

$$\{(\text{Forward Rate}) - (\text{Spot Rate})\}/(\text{Spot Rate}) = (\% \text{ change})$$

and is calculated as

$$\{(1.919) - (1.900)\}/(1.900) = 0.01$$

which is the monthly premium. Since there are 12 months in a year, the annual premium is 12 percent. If the spot rate exceeds the forward rate, then the calculated percentage change is negative and is called a discount.

Forward contracts are not always appropriate for, or even available to, some businesses and individuals. In the case of our lumber exporter, we should consider the possibility that the sale might fall through or that the Japanese importer might default. Then the exporter would be obligated to fulfill a foreign exchange obligation for which no currency is coming in. To fulfill the foreign exchange contract, the exporter would have to buy yen in the spot market three months later and bear the risk that he would have to pay more dollars for the yen than he would receive from his forward contract.

The bank is also in a risky position. Banks usually offset their forward exchange obligations with reverse forward contracts or, as we shall see in later chapters, by hedging in the international money market. In the event that one of their forward exchange contracts defaults, they are exposed to the same exchange rate risk as the exporter whose sale defaults. As a result, banks typically require collateral from the other party in forward exchange contracts unless they are dealing with large corporations or banks with outstanding credit ratings. Banks almost always refuse unsecured forward exchange contracts with individuals. Therefore, many businesses and most individuals must seek alternatives to forward exchange contracts.

CURRENCY FUTURES MARKETS

One alternative to a forward exchange contract is a currency futures contract. Like forward contracts, futures contracts specify the exchange of specified amounts of two currencies at a specified time in the future. However, currency futures can be bought and sold by most businesses and individuals. Furthermore, individuals and businesses can easily resell their currency futures contracts in the futures market, so the contracts do not have to be held to maturity.

A currency futures contract sold in the U.S. will specify that the owner will pay a fixed dollar price for a specified quantity of a foreign currency at a specified date. If the dollar value of the foreign currency rises, the value of a futures contract that enables the owner to purchase the currency at the lower fixed price will rise by an amount equal to the difference in the prices times the amount of currency specified. For example, if you own a futures contract that specifies the delivery of 125,000 deutsche marks at a price of $0.50 per mark, and the value of a mark rises to $0.51, your futures contract will increase in value by $1,250 = (0.01) (125,000).

In some ways the difference between a forward rate contract and a currency futures contract is analogous to the difference between a bank loan and commercial paper or bonds. Bank loans are contracts between the bank and the borrower. Terms are negotiable. If the borrower wants to pay off the loan early, the bank dictates the terms of repayment. The same is true with a forward rate contract. The terms are negotiable, but the bank must agree if the customer wants to void the contract prior to maturity. On the other hand, if a borrower sells securities such as commercial paper or bonds, the terms of the "loan" are nonnegotiable. Lenders either buy the securities or they don't. Either party can escape its obligation by buying back or selling the security in the secondary market. Futures are like bonds and commercial paper in the sense that they are "securitized forward contracts"; the terms are nonnegotiable and either party can escape the obligation by buying or selling the security in the secondary market.

Futures Versus Forward Contracts

In 1972, the Chicago Mercantile Exchange (CME), which has organized trading in commodities futures since 1919, established the International Monetary Market (IMM) for trading in currency futures contracts. An objective of the exchange was to provide a market in which investors and companies could quickly resell their futures contracts before maturity. The solution to providing an ongoing market for futures contracts is to standardize the contract and guarantee performance.

While forward contracts are only as good as the willingness of the two parties to fulfill their obligations, the CME guarantees the performance of the two parties in a futures contract. In fact, the buyer and seller of a futures contract are not aware of each other's identity. From their standpoint, they are dealing only with the CME. To control its risk exposure, the CME requires that buyers and sellers of futures contracts maintain a minimum *margin requirement* with their broker. A margin requirement is a cash deposit that must be maintained by the customer. The CME computes gains and losses on the market value of the futures contracts daily and subtracts or adds to the margin deposit. If the margin falls below the specified minimum, the investor must deposit additional funds to maintain the contract.

From the standpoint of the investor or business, futures contracts are superior to forward contracts because they eliminate the risk of default by the other party to the contract. In addition, margin requirements are only a small fraction of the collateral required on a forward contract. The disadvantage of futures contracts is that losses must be paid in cash daily, while losses on a forward contract are deferred until maturity. For example, if you have a forward contract to buy yen at a specific price and the market price of yen falls, you do not have to bear the loss until the contract matures and you have to pay the higher forward rate for yen. If, on the other hand, you have a futures contract to purchase yen at the same price, the value of the futures contract falls as the market price of yen falls, and you must bear the loss daily by depositing additional cash in order to maintain the minimum margin requirement.

To assure a sufficient volume of identical contracts for continuous trading, the CME standardizes futures contracts with respect to the maturity of the contract and the amount of the foreign currency. All U.S. futures contracts obligate the owner to buy an amount of foreign currency at a dollar price. This is sometimes referred to as taking delivery of the foreign currency. Settlement dates for currency futures fall on the third Wednesday of either March, June, September, or December. The amount of currency depends upon the type of currency. For example, typical futures contracts specify 62,500 British pounds per contract, 100,000 Canadian dollars per contract, 125,000 German marks per contract, and 12,500,000 Japanese yen per contract. Although the dollar value of one of these contracts is measured in tens of thousands of dollars, the customer's margin requirement is usually less than $2,000.

While the standardization of futures contracts assures a volume of identical contracts that is sufficient to maintain continuous trading, it forces investors and businesses to contract for specific amounts and delivery dates; whereas forward exchange contracts can be tailored to individual preferences for amounts and delivery dates. Still, the customers must pay for this convenience. Bid/ask spreads in the forward market are substantially greater than spreads and commissions in the futures market. Furthermore, the spread and commission encountered when buying a futures contract is virtually the same spread encountered if the contract must be sold before maturity. However, very few futures contracts are held to maturity. On the other hand, one must often pay an enormous spread if a forward contract must be sold or canceled before maturity. Therefore, forward contracts are usually held until maturity.

Trading Currency Futures

Because futures contracts specify only the purchase of foreign currency, investors and businesses that want to trade currency futures must be familiar with both long and short positions. When you *purchase* a futures contract, you have taken a *long position*. If you *sell* a futures contract, you have taken a *short position*. The futures exchange clears all investors's positions overnight, with long and short positions canceling one another. For example, if at the end of the trading day you have purchased 10 futures contracts and sold six, you will begin the next day in a long position of four contracts. If you sold more contracts than you purchased, you would begin the next day in a short position.

Speculators who expect a currency to increase in value want to buy a currency futures contract and be in a long position, since the value of the contract rises as the value of the currency rises. They would want to sell the futures contract and be in a short position if they expect the value of the currency to fall. Since short positions are unfamiliar to many investors, the following example traces the experience of a currency futures short seller.

Consider an investor in early January 1992 who believes that the dollar value of the British pound will fall below $1.60 over the next three months. A check of currency futures prices in *The Wall Street Journal* reveals that the March futures contract for pounds sold for $1.9050 per pound. The investor's broker explains that the March futures contract for pounds requires delivery of 62,500 pounds on the third Wednesday in March. The initial margin required from the investor is $2,000 and the maintenance margin is $1,500.

Because our investor believes the value of the pound will decline, she can expect to profit by selling the futures contract. If she expected the value of the pound to increase, she would want to buy the futures contract. Therefore, she deposits $2,000 initial margin and instructs her broker to sell short one March futures contract for British pounds at $1.9040 or better. Since this is a short sale, the instruction to sell at $1.9040 or better means that the broker will make the sale only at a futures price greater than or equal to $1.9040. The broker charges her $15 commission and instructs a floor trader at the IMM to sell one futures contract. The trader on the floor of the exchange offers to sell and finds a buyer at $1.9048.

Suppose that at the end of the day the last trade in pound futures takes place at $1.9030. The IMM acts as a clearing house and *marks to market* all future contracts. It electronically exchanges all investor contracts for new contracts at a price of

$1.9030 per pound. Our investor's short position in the pound at $1.9048 is exchanged for a new short position at a price of $1.9030, and the IMM credits the gain of $0.0018 per pound on 62,500 pounds or (0.0018 * 62,500) = $112.50 to her account. If she wishes, she may withdraw the $112.50 the next day.

The next day the contract opens at $1.9030. Suppose the futures price then closes up at $1.9160. The IMM will then mark all contracts to market. The loss of (1.9160 − 1.9030) = 0.0130 per pound that will result is a deduction of (0.0130 * 62,500) = $812.50 from our investor's account. This results in a balance of (2,112.50 − 812.50) = $1,300, which is below the required maintenance balance of $1,500. Our investor will receive a *margin call*, which requires her to bring the balance up to $1,500 by depositing $200. If she fails to deposit the $200, the contract will be closed out and her account reduced to $1,300 less any additional loss the next day.

Suppose our investor meets the margin call by depositing the $200 but has lost confidence and wishes to close out the position the next day. She does so by buying one March futures contract for pounds. No additional deposit is required. At the end of the day, the IMM clearing house matches the long and short positions in a customer's account and cancels both contracts. As noted previously, most futures contracts are cleared in this manner. Less than one percent are held to maturity. Speculators do not need to take delivery of the foreign currency in order to cash in their profits. The overnight clearing operation converts gains and losses into cash on a daily basis.

CHAPTER PERSPECTIVE

The bid/ask spread constitutes the cost of exchanging currencies. The bid rate is the price a dealer is offering to pay for a currency; the ask rate is the price a dealer is willing to sell a currency for. The size of the spread between the bid and ask rate depends on the risks and costs incurred by currency dealers and is restricted by the potential for locational arbitrage.

Three basic contracts govern the exchange of currencies. Spot exchange contracts refer to the immediate exchange of currencies. Forward exchange contracts refer to the exchange of specific amounts of currency at some time in the future. Currency futures contracts are standardized and guaranteed forward contracts that are traded on the IMM. Each type of currency exchange contract offers particular advantages and disadvantages to both businesses and investors.

Currency Options

INTRODUCTION AND MAIN POINTS

In Chapter 3, we examined the three basic contracts used to exhange currencies: spot contracts, forward contracts, and futures contracts. This chapter explores the nature and use of options contracts.

It is useful to view an option simply as a more complex contract governing the exchange of currencies. We begin by describing the nature of an option contract, along with its many variations and uses. We conclude with a discussion of the principles underlying the valuation of options.

After studying the material in this chapter:

━━ You will understand the nature of an option contract.

━━ You will be able to distinguish the varieties of option contracts.

━━ You will be familiar with the operations of currency option markets.

━━ You will understand the general economic uses of both put and call options on currencies.

━━ You will recognize the costs and risks associated with the use of currency options.

━━ You will understand the economics underlying the determination of option premiums.

CURRENCY OPTIONS

Forward and futures contracts obligate the investor to exchange specific amounts of two currencies at a specified time in the future. The investor must make the exchange even if the transaction is disadvantageous. Many investors prefer to be in the position of having the right to exchange the currencies but not the obligation. If the transaction turns out to be advantageous, they can compel the exchange of currencies. But, if the transaction turns out to be unfavorable, they can simply decline to exchange the currencies.

A contract that specifies such an enviable arrangement is called an option; so called because the investor has the option (not the obligation) to make the exchange. The disadvantage of an option contract is that the investor must pay a substantial premium to induce the other party to sign the contract.

Terminology of Options

An option to buy 31,250 British pounds in three months at a price of $1.90 per pound assigns to the owner of the option a right to buy 31,250 pounds from the ~~writer of the option~~. This right is contingent on the payment of $1.90 per pound. Because the owner of an option cannot exercise his right to the pounds without making the payment, the price of $1.90 per pound is called the ~~exercise price (or striking price)~~ of the option. ~~The time at which the contingent claim expires is called the~~ *maturity* ~~of the option.~~

The *~~intrinsic value~~* of an option is the ~~difference between what one would pay (market exchange rate) for a currency without the option and what one would pay (the exercise price) with the option~~. For example, suppose the pound is currently selling for $2.00. The intrinsic value of the option is $0.10 per pound (= 2.00 − 1.90). Because an option does not have to be exercised, its intrinsic value can never be negative. If the market price of the pound is less than $1.90 per pound, the option's intrinsic value is zero.

~~The *premium* on an option is the difference between the market price of the option and its intrinsic value~~. For example, if the option is selling for $0.15 per pound, its premium is $0.05 per pound (= 0.15 − 0.10).

TRADED CURRENCY OPTIONS

Any two parties may create a currency option contract that specifies whatever quantity, maturity, and exercise price they desire. Some banks will tailor individual currency options for their best corporate customers. However, each party has little choice but to hold these options until maturity unless it can find a mutually agreeable replacement.

When the volume of contingent claims is sufficient, it is possible to organize a secondary market for trading in option contracts in a manner similar to that for organized trading in futures contracts. In the U.S., the Chicago Board of Trade (CBT) conducts organized trading in stock options, while the Philadelphia Stock Exchange conducts organized trading in currency options.

A closely related option on currency futures contracts is traded on the International Monetary Market of the CME. Although the CME option is on the currency futures contract itself, rather than the currency, there is little practical difference to options traders.

There is now an organized market for trading currency options in London. These options are known as European options, and they can only be exercised at maturity. This contrasts with American options, which can be exercised prior to maturity. Although European and American options on stocks are valued differently, there is little difference in the valuation of European and American currency options.

As is true with futures contracts, *exchange-traded options* require standardized contracts and guarantees of performance. Currency options expire on the Friday before the third Wednesday of the month. The amount of currency involved in each contract is one-half the amount of the futures contract. The guarantor of performance is the Options Clearing Corporation. Currency futures options are matched to the characteristics of the futures contract and guaranteed by the IMM.

PUT VERSUS CALL OPTIONS

There are two basic types of option contracts. ~~Call options bestow upon their owner the right to buy at a particular date in the future a specified amount of foreign currency at a specified price.~~ *Put options* ~~give their owner the right to sell at a particular date in the future a specified amount of foreign currency at a specified price.~~

If you exercise a call option, you must pay the *exercise price*, which is sometimes called the *striking price*. If you exercise a put option, you receive the exercise (striking) price. The other party to an option, who is obligated to perform at the behest of the owner of the option, is called the *writer of the option*. One writes options in order to receive the premium on the option, which is paid by the owner of the option.

Consider an investor who believes in January that the value of the pound will rise from its current value of $1.95 to over $2.10 within six months. He knows that there is a possibility that the value of the pound will suddenly drop. Because he has limited financial resources, he does not want to take the risk of buying a pound futures contract. He calls his broker and asks about call options on British pounds that mature in June. (If our investor believes that the pound will fall in value, he would be interested in put options.) The broker informs the investor that a call option with an exercise price of $2.00 is currently selling at a premium of $0.0350. Since the exercise price and premium are quoted in dollars per pound, he tells his broker to buy one call option and pays (31,250 * 0.035) = $1,093.75 plus $25 commission.

If the spot price of the pound rises as the option matures, the option will increase in value. If the spot price decreases, the value of the option will decrease. However, our investor will never be asked to deposit additional money. He can never lose more than his initial investment. Only option writers are exposed to the risk of indeterminate losses; therefore, only option writers are required to satisfy margin or collateral requirements.

Although currency options can be held to maturity and exercised, their owners generally sell them prior to maturity. Suppose the value of the pound rises to $2.10 in April. The investor does not have the option of exercising before maturity. The intrinsic value of the option is the market value of the pound less the exercise price, $(2.10 - 2.00) = \$0.10$ per pound or $(0.10 * 31,250) = \$3,125$. But options will usually sell for more than their intrinsic value, so our investor can simply sell the option before maturity.

DETERMINANTS OF OPTION PRICES

Figure 4-1 graphs both the price and the intrinsic value of a currency call option as a function of the expected spot exchange rate at maturity. Both the intrinsic value and price are quoted in dollars per unit of foreign currency. We determine the actual value and price that must be paid by multiplying the number of foreign currency units specified in the option contract. The intrinsic value of the option equals the current spot rate minus the exercise price but is never less than zero, since an investor does not have to exercise the option. Hence, the solid line—representing intrinsic value—runs along the horizontal axis, indicating a value of zero, until the spot rate exceeds the exercise price (X). Each penny increase in the spot rate increases the intrinsic value of the option by one penny, so the line depicting intrinsic value rises at a ratio of one to one for spot rates that exceed the exercise price.

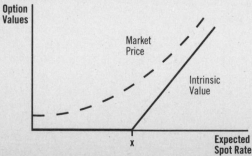

Fig. 4-1 *Value of call options*

The dashed line represents the market price of the option. At all levels of the spot rate, the price of the option exceeds the intrinsic value. The difference between the price that investors are willing to pay for an option and its intrinsic value equals the *premium* on the option.

Investors are willing to pay premiums for options because there is a potential for large profits if the exchange rate rises, while the losses are limited if the exchange rate falls. The premium on the option is greatest when the spot rate is equal to the exercise price.

When the spot rate is below the exercise price, there is a lower probability that it will rise above the exercise price, which reduces the premium. The premium is also reduced when the spot rate is above the exercise price because the price of the option, which is the amount the option owner invests and may lose, is greater.

The maturity of the option and the volatility in the value of the underlying foreign currency also influence the option premium. Investors will pay more for an option with a longer maturity because a longer waiting period increases the probability that the exchange rate will exceed the exercise price. Similarly, a more volatile currency also has a greater probability of rising above the exercise price.

Figure 4-2 depicts the intrinsic value and market price of a put option as a function of the expected future spot price. Put options have value only when the spot rate falls below the exercise price. The intrinsic value is the exercise price minus the exchange rate. For spot rates above the exercise price, the intrinsic value is zero rather than negative because the owner of the option will simply choose not to exercise it.

Fig. 4-2 *Value of put options*

As is true with call options, the market price of a put option generally exceeds its intrinsic value. Investors are willing to pay a premium on put options for the same reasons that they are willing to pay premiums on call options. Their potential gains from changes in the exchange rate prior to maturity of the option exceed their potential losses, which are limited to their initial investment. The premium is greatest when the exchange rate equals the exercise price and is an increasing function of both the maturity of the option and the volatility in the value of the underlying foreign currency.

WHO BENEFITS FROM CURRENCY OPTIONS?

Currency speculators like options because they offer unlimited potential gains, while strictly limiting losses. However, if owning the option is such a good deal, why would anyone be willing to write one? The answer is that the premium that the writer receives must be worth the risk of potentially unlimited losses.

So why should anyone engage in currency option contracts? Investors can benefit if they have information about future changes in exchange rates that no one else has, in which case others will be willing to write options in return for inadequate premiums.

Although companies might possibly benefit from this type of information, they usually use options for a different purpose. Consider a U.S. company that knows it will receive 31,250 pounds in three months. The business is subject to potential insolvency if the value of the pound falls below $1.90. The costs of insolvency are much greater than any actual loss associated with the value of the 31,250 pounds; hence the business will be willing to pay a substantial premium in order to avoid the possibility of insolvency.

CHAPTER PERSPECTIVE

Currency futures contracts are standardized and guaranteed forward contracts that are traded on the IMM. Currency options are similar to futures contracts with the exception that the owner of the option can choose whether to actually carry out the currency exchange. Currency options can specify either the right to sell a currency or the right to buy a currency. In order to induce someone to write an option, the owner of the option must pay a premium. This premium is a function of the difference between the exercise price and the currency's value, the variability of the currency's value, and the maturity of the option. The trade-off between the premium on the option and the potentially unlimited gains that it offers governs their usefulness.

Determining Floating Exchange Rates

INTRODUCTION AND MAIN POINTS

Managers and investors need more than an understanding of exchange rates and the various types of currency exchange contracts in order to deal effectively with currency risks. They must be able to anticipate changes in exchange rates. Without a grasp of the fundamental forces and mechanisms behind exchange rate changes, they cannot hope to foresee and forestall potential currency risks. In this chapter, we focus on the market price concept of exchange rates. We examine international trade and credit factors that influence the supply and demand for currency in foreign exchange markets and explain how they can be used to understand and forecast exchange rate changes.

After studying the material in this chapter:

■ You will be able to relate changes in international trade to fluctuations in currency values.

■ You will understand the influence of international credit markets on foreign exchange prices.

■ You will be able to anticipate the impact of international lending and investment on trade patterns and currency markets.

■ You will understand the use of balance of payments concepts as they are used to forecast exchange rates.

FOREIGN TRADE

In Chapter 2, the concept of a market price was used to define an exchange rate; imports into a country create a supply of its currency in the foreign exchange market, while exports out of a country create a demand for its currency. In this chapter we expand the analysis of foreign trade influences on the foreign exchange market and show how to use the insights obtained to forecast changes in exchange rates.

Effect of Imports

Imports of foreign goods and services into the U.S. create a supply of dollars on the foreign exchange market. It does not matter which country the imports originate from. If the imports are from Japan, dollars are supplied in exchange for yen to pay the Japanese suppliers. If the imports are from Germany, dollars are supplied in exchange for deutsche marks to pay the German suppliers. The same is true for any currency. British imports create a supply of pounds. French imports create a supply of francs. The point is that imports into any country create a supply of its currency on the foreign exchange market.

Figure 5-1 demonstrates the general effect of an increase in imports on a currency's value (exchange rate). An increase in imports creates an increased supply of the currency at all levels of the exchange rate, represented by a movement of the supply curve to the right. The new exchange rate is the lower *equilibrium rate* at which the supply of the currency equals the demand for the currency.

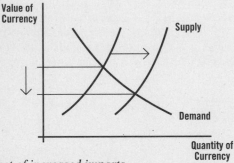

Fig. 5-1 *Effect of increased imports*

A reduction in imports decreases the supply of a country's currency, shifting the supply curve to the left and leading to an increase in the value of the currency.

Forecasts of exchange rate changes can be based upon any factors that can increase or decrease a country's imports. For example, a recession in the U.S. lowers demand for imports along with domestic goods and services. Reduced imports in turn decrease the supply of dollars on the foreign exchange market. We would therefore expect the exchange rate of the dollar to rise. On the other hand, a tax cut would be expected to increase demand for imports, which in turn would be expected to lead to a decline in the value of the dollar.

In general, any factor, such as the business cycle, taxes, tariffs, import quotas, crop failures, technological innovations, or government regulations, that might affect imports can be used to develop forecasts of exchange rate changes. It is necessary simply to determine the effect of the factor on imports and analyze the effect on the supply and demand for the currency.

Effect of Exports

Exports of goods and services from a country create a demand for its currency on the foreign exchange market. It does not matter to which country the exports are going. American producers of goods and services want to be paid in dollars. Foreign consumers of American goods and services must exchange their foreign currencies for dollars in order to make payment, so American exports create a demand for dollars in the foreign exchange market. Likewise, when Americans consume German goods and services, they must demand deutsche marks in the foreign exchange market in order to pay the German producers.

As shown in Figure 5-2, a reduction in exports at all levels of the exchange rate causes the demand curve for the currency to shift to the left, which results in a lower equilibrium exchange rate. Conversely, an increase in a country's exports would lead to a rise in the value of its currency, since the demand curve would shift to the right.

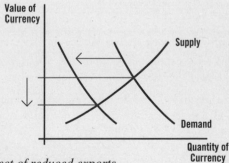

Fig. 5-2 *Effect of reduced exports*

Factors that influence exports can also be used to forecast exchange rate changes. For example, crop failures overseas would cause large increases in American grain exports. Accordingly, the demand for dollars at all levels of the exchange rate would increase and we would anticipate an increase in the value of the dollar. On the other hand, labor strikes in the American aerospace industry would reduce exports, putting downward pressure on the dollar. Hence, any factor that influences the amount of a country's exports at all levels of the exchange rate can be used when forecasting future exchange rates.

Interactions of Imports and Exports

The effects of imports and exports interact in the determination of the exchange rate. Suppose massive crop failures overseas produce a dramatic increase in American grain exports. In the absence of other effects, the resulting increase in the value of the dollar would lower the dollar price of foreign imports to American consumers. The lower price would induce more demand for imported goods; hence, imports would increase until the supply of dollars equaled the demand for dollars on the foreign exchange market.

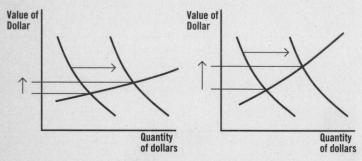

Fig. 5-3 *Relationship between currency value and supply*

Figure 5-3 shows that the magnitude of the rise in the value of the dollar depends on the slope of the supply curve for the dollar. The effect of increasing grain exports is to shift the demand curve to the right. The consequent increase in imports is depicted by the movement along the supply curve. The slope of the supply curve indicates how sensitive the magnitude of imports is to changes in the value of the dollar. A higher slope means that a given increase in the value of the dollar induces a smaller increase in imports.

Just as the magnitude of the effect of an increase in exports on the exchange rate depends upon the sensitivity of imports to the exchange rate, the magnitude of the effect of an increase in imports depends upon the sensitivity of exports to the exchange rate. For example, suppose the United States government imposes a restrictive textile quota, which reduces imports. The reduction in imports at all levels of the exchange rate can be viewed as a shift to the left in the supply curve, which increases the value of the dollar. The higher value of the dollar in turn increases the foreign price of American exports. The magnitude of the resulting decrease in exports depends upon the sensitivity of exports to the exchange rate.

The sensitivity of a country's imports and exports to changes in price depends upon the availability of competitive alternatives. If a country has domestic substitutes for its imports, then a small increase in the price of the imports is likely to have a large effect on the amount of imports. If many countries compete to export the same goods and services, then the amount of exports will be very sensitive to small changes in the exchange rate. For example, a technologically advanced country such as Japan exports many manufactured goods for which substitutes from other countries are not readily available. The quantity of Japan's exports is not very sensitive to changes in the value of the yen. On the other hand, an agricultural exporting country such as Argentina would experience a dramatic reduction in exports if the value of the austral rose, since agricultural commodities are readily available for export from other countries.

INTERNATIONAL CREDIT

Many factors besides foreign trade in goods and services influence the exchange rate. International borrowing, lending, and investment also create a supply or demand for currencies on the foreign exchange market. In terms of the amounts of currency exchanged in recent decades, international credit flows dwarf all other factors that create supply and demand for currencies on the foreign exchange market. The following sections explore the effect of credit flows.

Foreign Borrowing

If you wish to purchase more goods and services than you can pay for, you must borrow from another individual, business, or government agency. When Americans borrow domestically, someone who chooses to purchase fewer goods and services than he can pay for in dollars, transfers some of his dollars to the borrower. This can be done directly or indirectly through a wide variety of public and private financial intermediaries.

When Americans borrow from foreigners, someone in a foreign country who chooses to purchase fewer goods and services than he can pay for in his currency transfers some of that foreign currency to the American borrower. Unless the American borrower chooses to purchase goods and services in the country of the foreign lender, the foreign currency must be converted in the foreign exchange market. The currency of the borrower is demanded, and the currency of the lender is supplied.

Consider an American corporation that wants to borrow $100 million from a Japanese bank. The Japanese bank could convert 13 billion yen of its Japanese depositors' savings into dollars at an exchange rate of 13 yen per dollar and make a $100-million loan. On the other hand, the Japanese bank could lend the American corporation 13 billion yen. The American firm would then convert the yen into dollars in the foreign exchange market. In either case, the effect of American borrowing from Japan would be an increased demand for dollars at all levels of the exchange rate.

Figure 5-4 shows that the effect of the increased demand for dollars is to raise the yen value of the dollar on the foreign exchange market. The country from which Americans borrow does not matter. Anytime Americans borrow from other countries, the demand for dollars in the overseas exchange market is increased, which tends to increase the value of the dollar.

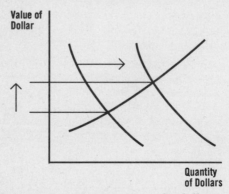

Fig. 5-4 *Effect of American borrowing on the dollar*

Factors that increase foreign borrowing can justify forecasts of increases in the foreign exchange value of the borrower's currency. Factors that decrease foreign borrowing can justify forecasts of lower currency values.

For example, if an increase in the U.S. Government's deficit is not met by either a reduction in private domestic borrowing or increased domestic saving, the deficit will be financed by increased foreign borrowing. Massive increases in the federal deficit in the early 1980s were accompanied by a dramatic rise in the value of the dollar. Other things being equal, a reduction in the federal deficit would tend to lower the value of the dollar.

Foreign Lending

In the previous section, we saw that the effect on the foreign exchange market of American borrowing from Japan is to increase the demand for the dollar. At the same time, however, the foreign exchange market will experience an increased supply of Japanese yen. When individuals, businesses, or governments in one country lend to those in a foreign country, the foreign exchange market experiences an increased supply of the lender's currency. It does not matter which foreign country receives the funds. The currency of the lender will ultimately be supplied in exchange for the borrower's currency.

Figure 5-5 shows the effect of an American loan of $100 million to a utility company in France. It does not matter whether the bank lends francs or dollars. If it lends dollars, the French company will supply them to the foreign exchange market in return for francs. If the bank lends francs, it must first supply 100 million of its depositors' dollars to the foreign exchange market in return for francs. The effect on exchange rates is the same. An increased supply of dollars lowers the value of the dollar in francs.

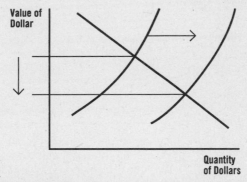

Fig. 5-5 *Effect of American lending on the dollar*

Factors that can affect the amount of foreign lending can also form the basis of forecasts for changes in the exchange rate. For example, during the 1970s American banks lent hundreds of billions of dollars to Latin America. In the early 1980s, many of the major debtor countries in Latin America had difficulty servicing their American bank debt. As a result, most American banks refused to lend additional funds to these countries. This large reduction in foreign lending contributed to the massive run-up in the value of the dollar in the early 1980s.

INTERACTION OF TRADE AND CREDIT

The effects of foreign trade and credit transactions can interact in the determination of the exchange rate. Consider the effect of a large U.S. Government deficit that is financed by foreign investors. The effect of the foreign borrowing in the foreign exchange market is to shift the demand curve for the dollar to the right.

The increased demand raises the value of the dollar, which in turn reduces the dollar price of foreign imports into the U.S. and raises the foreign currency price of American exports to other countries. Consequently, American imports increase and American exports decrease. The magnitude of the rise in the value of the dollar depends upon the relative sensitivity of imports and exports to changes in the value of the dollar.

BALANCE OF PAYMENTS

International credit flows can completely offset the effect of international trade on the exchange rate. A large increase in imports can be financed by borrowing from the exporting country. Similarly, a country can lend the funds to another country to finance exports to that country. For example, if the U.S. borrows $1 billion from Japanese banks to finance the import of $1 billion worth of Japanese steel, there will be no effect on the exchange rate, since the import creates a supply of dollars on the foreign exchange market, while the loan creates an equal demand for dollars.

In the absence of government intervention, exchange rates will adjust so that imbalances between imports and exports are exactly offset by an appropriate international credit flow. A net trade surplus will be offset by net foreign lending; a net trade deficit will be offset by net foreign borrowing. If trade surpluses/deficits are not matched by foreign lending/borrowing, then the supply and demand for currency on the foreign exchange market will not be equal.

This relationship between net trade and net credit flows constitutes the basis of the *balance of payments* accounts. When governments wish to maintain or stabilize exchange rates at fixed levels, they must act to make up any imbalance in the net trade and credit flows. Otherwise the exchange rate will move to a new market price at which the supply and demand for the currency is equal. The means by which countries make up these imbalances are explored in Chapter 6.

CHAPTER PERSPECTIVE

This chapter explores the economic factors that induce changes in exchange rates. Because exchange rates are market prices of one currency in terms of another, changes in exchange rates can be attributed to changes in the supply and demand for the currency on the foreign exchange market.

Growth in exports of goods and services increase the demand for a country's currency, which causes the value of the currency to rise. A reduction in exports induces a fall in the currency's value.

Expanded investment and borrowing from foreign countries increases demand for a country's currency, which causes the exchange rate to rise. Lending and investment in foreign countries increases the supply of a country's currency, which causes the exchange rate to fall.

The magnitude of the increase or decrease in the value of a country's currency depends upon the sensitivity of a country's imports and exports to changes in the exchange rate. The sensitivity of imports and exports to the exchange rate in turn depends upon the availability of competitive alternatives to the goods and services that are being imported and exported.

Government Intervention in Currency Markets

INTRODUCTION AND MAIN POINTS

In Chapter 5, we examined the economic forces that influence exchange rates through supply and demand for the currency in the foreign exchange market. In this chapter, we examine the influence of governments on exchange rates. Governments can regulate the value of their currency, buy and sell large amounts of currency in the foreign exchange market, pursue economic policies that will influence the supply and demand for their currency, and enter into international agreements concerning exchange rates.

After studying the material in this chapter:

■■ You will be able to anticipate the existence of advantageous black market and offshore exchange rates.

■■ You will understand the methods and limitations of government intervention in the foreign exchange market.

■■ You will be familiar with reserve currencies and special international currency reserves such as Special Drawing Rights and European Currency Units.

■■ You will be able to analyze the effect of monetary and fiscal policies on currency values.

■■ You will understand the nature and function of systems of international exchange rate regulation such as the Bretton Woods System and European Monetary System.

LEGAL, BLACK MARKET, AND OFFSHORE RATES

Exchange rates that float according to private economic forces of supply and demand in the currency markets can be economically destabilizing. Large fluctuations in exchange rates can create boom-and-bust cycles in industries that export or that are subject to competition from imports. This often results in political pressure for governments to stabilize or influence exchange rates.

The simplest method of exchange rate regulation is for a government to pass a law that prohibits the exchange of currency at a rate other than one that is officially determined by the government.

These kinds of regulated exchange rates are called *official* or *legal exchange rates*. The official rate of exchange is usually set in terms of a major reserve currency. Most less developed countries tie their currencies to the dollar; however many former colonies of Britain and France tie their currencies to the pound and franc, respectively; *cross rates* (see Chapter 2) then determine the official exchange rates vis-à-vis other currencies.

Sometimes governments have several different legal rates for currency exchange, depending on the reason given for the exchange. For example, foreign businesses that wish to invest inside the country may be offered a more favorable exchange rate than tourists or citizens who wish to invest outside the country. In the case of some very large or irregular transactions, some governments, particularly in Latin America and Africa, negotiate an official rate for that particular transaction. However, such instances are rare.

The problem with official exchange rates is that there is almost always either an excess demand or an excess supply of the currency at the offical price. When the official rate is below the market rate, people can sell as much currency as they like in exchange for other currencies, but cannot buy as much as they want. When the official rate is above the market price, the situation is reversed. If there is an excess supply or demand, individuals have an incentive to convert the currency illegally at a *black market exchange rate*. The black market rate is higher than the official rate when there is an excess demand for the currency at the official rate and lower when there is an excess supply.

If the excess supply or demand for a currency at an official rate is of sufficient magnitude, trading at unofficial rates may take place in another country. The term *offshore exchange rate* describes the rate at which such transactions take place. The usefulness of the offshore currency exchange is limited, however, because countries that proscribe currency exchange at unofficial rates almost always restrict the movement of currency in and out of the country.

MARKET INTERVENTION

Because of the difficulties associated with official exchange rates such as excess supply and demand, offshore exchange, and black markets, most major industrialized countries allow their exchange rates to float. A *floating exchange rate system* is one in which governments allow the conversion of currencies at whatever rate the market determines.

Two problems confront governments that allow their currencies to float. First, the variability of the exchange rate introduces additional uncertainties into international transactions. Second, large movements in exchange rates can create boom-and-bust cycles in industries that are subject to foreign competition.

In order to alleviate these difficulties, most governments intervene in the foreign exchange market in an attempt to stabilize currency values. This intervention by governments in the foreign exchange market has led some to refer to the current exchange rate system as a *dirty float*. This contrasts with a free floating system in which only private economic forces influence the market.

Reserves

The simplest form of intervention in the foreign exchange market entails the purchase or sale by the government of large amounts of currency. Because an excess supply of a country's currency causes its value to fall, the government can maintain the value of the currency by purchasing the excess supply. Conversely, a government can prevent a run-up in the value of its currency by selling enough to satisfy the excess demand.

The purchase or sale of currency requires the government to exchange the currency for something else. Most often the government receives or pays out other currencies. Hence, countries that intervene in the foreign exchange market maintain substantial foreign currency reserves. The most widely used reserve currency is the U.S. dollar. However, other major currencies, such as the British pound, Japanese yen, and German deutsche mark, are also used as reserve currencies.

Although governments usually buy and sell currency with other currencies, there are alternatives. A government can use its gold reserves to purchase its currency and add to its gold reserves when it sells its currency. Governments can also purchase their currencies with *Special Drawing Rights* (SDRs). Special Drawing Rights are created by the International Monetary Fund and issued to member countries. The value of an SDR is a weighted average of the value of the currencies of the major industrial countries. A weighted average differs from a simple average in which all currencies have equal influence in determining the average value. The value of major currencies such as the dollar are weighted more heavily in determining the average.

SDRs and gold play the same role in maintaining stable exchange rates. The advantage of using SDRs is that countries can avoid having to accumulate expensive gold reserves.

Members of the European Monetary System may also exchange *European Currency Units* (ECUs) for their currencies. Like the SDR, the ECU is equivalent to a weighted average of the currencies of countries that are members of the European Monetary System. The greatest weight is assigned to the deutsche mark.

INDIRECT INTERVENTION

Instead of intervening directly in the foreign exchange market by buying and selling currencies, governments can intervene indirectly by taking actions that induce others to buy or sell in the foreign exchange market. The three major forms of indirect intervention are monetary policy, fiscal policy, and jawboning.

Monetary Policy

Intervention by a government through purchases and sales of currency in the foreign exchange market is limited by the size of the government's reserves. An indirect but more powerful form of intervention involves the use of monetary policy by the country's central bank to vary domestic interest rates.

For example, if the Federal Reserve wants to halt a decline in the value of the dollar, it can sell U.S. Treasury bills via its open market operations. The added supply of T-bills will depress their price, in turn raising their interest rate. Higher interest rates in the United States will attract foreign lenders to U.S. securities and reduce American investment abroad. American borrowing from foreigners will increase, creating additional demand for dollars in the foreign exchange market, and American lending to foreigners will decrease, reducing the supply of dollars in the foreign exchange market. The increased demand and reduced supply of dollars in the foreign exchange market will increase the value of the dollar.

Conversely, if the Federal Reserve wants to reduce the value of the dollar, it can buy T-bills. The reduced supply of T-bills will reduce U.S. interest rates, and the value of the dollar will fall as U.S. investors pursue higher interest rates overseas and foreign investors lend less in the United States.

A serious disadvantage of using monetary policy to influence the exchange rate is that the same open market operations that increase or decrease interest rates also increase or decrease the domestic money supply, which is made up of currency in circulation and transaction deposits such as checking accounts at banks. Large changes in the domestic money supply can create inflation or deflation. The serious economic problems that can arise from inflation or deflation severely limit the freedom of the government to apply monetary policy to influence the exchange rate.

Fiscal Policy

Because of the problems that can result from using monetary policy to control the exchange rate, governments often use fiscal policy. Fiscal policy refers to changes in the level of taxation and government spending along with the budget deficits or surpluses that may result. In order to increase the value of its currency, a government may pursue a restrictive fiscal policy. An expansive fiscal policy, on the other hand, lowers the value of the currency.

A restrictive fiscal policy can be pursued by reducing the growth rate of expenditures or raising taxes, or both. Any deficit is reduced, and any surplus would be increased. A restrictive fiscal policy lowers overall demand for goods and services in the economy. This reduction in aggregate demand is reflected in a reduction in imports, which decreases the supply of the currency in the foreign exchange market, increasing the value of the currency.

An expansive fiscal policy has the opposite effect. Demand for goods and services is increased, and the supply of available domestic credit is reduced. Imports increase, which increases the supply of currency and causes the exchange rate to fall.

Jawboning

As is the case with monetary policy, the use of fiscal policy has other effects that are often unpopular with the public, such as increased taxes and reductions in or restrictions on the growth of government benefits. Hence, governments often resort to what has become known as jawboning.

Jawboning entails widely publicized pronouncements by high government officials that government will pursue a particular strategy concerning exchange rate movements. The intention of jawboning is to influence the expectations of foreign exchange traders concerning future exchange rates. For example, if the value of the dollar has declined for an extended period of time, foreign exchange traders may expect it to continue its decline. This expectation may lead them to sell their dollar assets in order to avoid continued losses. This additional selling of dollars can make the expectation self-fulfilling. In order to reduce or reverse this trend, the president, the secretary of the Treasury, and the chairman of the Federal Reserve may all make public pronouncements that it is public policy to prevent a continued decline.

Traders know that governments have the power to carry out their intention, if they are willing to pursue the required monetary, fiscal, and reserve policies. If traders believe that the government will indeed pursue the appropriate policies, then their expectation of continued decline in the value of the dollar will be changed. They will stop selling dollar assets, and the decline in the value of the dollar will be halted, without any need for the government to carry out the threatened policies.

The problem with jawboning is that it is effective only if foreign exchange traders believe that the government officials have the requisite power and will to carry out their promised monetary, fiscal, and reserve policies. Sadly, recent experience has shown that governments are often not up to the task. Hence, traders sometimes do not believe the public pronouncements, and jawboning becomes ineffective.

A good example of the limitations of public pronouncements by government officials occurred near the end of the Carter administration. Foreign central bankers refused to support the efforts of the Carter administration to raise the value of the dollar; confidence in the dollar was restored only when President Carter replaced Federal Reserve Chairman William Miller with Paul Volker, a monetary conservative whom the Carter administration had previously passed over for appointment as Fed chairman.

MULTINATIONAL ARRANGEMENTS

Government intervention in the foreign exchange market is more effective if it is coordinated with the efforts of other governments. For example, if the Japanese government is trying to reduce the value of the yen at the same time that the U.S. government is trying to raise the value of the dollar, then their efforts will support rather than offset each other and public pronouncements of their joint intention are much more likely to be believed by foreign exchange traders.

The degree of international coordination in regulating exchange rates varies widely. At times, countries have engaged in competitive devaluations in order to enhance exports, while at other times countries have entered into treaty arrangements to control exchange rates. In the following sections, we examine the existing European Monetary System, which governs currencies in the European Economic Community (EEC) with the exception of Britain. We also examine the gold standard and the Bretton Woods System. Although the gold standard and the Bretton Woods System are no longer in use, many economists and political leaders are now calling for a return to one or the other in order to avoid the economic instabilities associated with fluctuating exchange rates. Some movement toward these or similar arrangements seems likely in the future.

The Gold Standard

During the nineteenth and early twentieth centuries, most of the industrialized countries were on the *gold standard*. This meant that each country guaranteed the convertibility of its currency into a specific amount of gold. The guarantee meant that the government agreed to buy or sell any weight of gold from or to anyone at a fixed price per ounce in terms of its currency. Since each currency could be exchanged for a specified amount of gold, arbitrage set the exchange rate between two currencies to the ratio of their gold prices. For example, suppose the British government set the price of gold at 10 pounds per ounce and the U.S. government set the price of gold at $20 per ounce. Since

$$(dollars/ounce)/(pounds/ounce) = (dollars/pound)$$

The equilibrium exchange rate will be

$$(20)/(10) = (2)$$

or $2 per pound.

If the exchange rate is higher, such as $2.01 per pound, then arbitrageurs can buy gold from the U.S. for $20 per ounce, sell it to Britain for 10 pounds per ounce, and convert the pounds to $20.10, which gives them a profit of .10 per ounce. Since arbitrageurs would be supplying pounds in the foreign exchange market, the value of the pound would quickly fall to $2.00, which would eliminate the arbitrage profit.

On the other hand, if the exchange rate of the pound were less than $2 per pound, arbitrageurs could profit from buying British gold, sell it to the U.S., and exchange dollars for pounds. The demand for pounds would quickly raise the value of the pound to $2.

There are several problems with the gold standard. First, countries have to hold substantial gold reserves at considerable cost to taxpayers. Second, because there is no formal agreement among individual countries to maintain the price of gold, political pressures on governments to change the gold price of their currency or to suspend convertibility altogether are often irresistible.

Third, since all countries must hold gold reserves, there is a temptation to hoard or accumulate gold reserves during periods of uncertainty. These problems, along with others, led to the collapse of the gold standard prior to World War II.

Bretton Woods

Near the end of World War II, the U.S. and Great Britain began planning for a system of international exchange rate regulation that would improve upon the gold standard. They, along with most of the Western allied powers, signed an agreement that is known as the *Bretton Woods Agreement of 1944*. The major provisions of the agreement were the establishment of the *International Monetary Fund* (IMF) and the *World Bank* and the adoption of a system for stabilizing exchange rates.

A key feature of the Bretton Woods System was that each country agreed to maintain a fixed dollar value of its currency, called the currency's *parity rate*. This required each country to hold dollars as a reserve currency and use them to buy their own currency when its dollar value fell and sell their own currency when its dollar value rose. As a result, the exchange rate for all currencies other than the dollar were fixed by triangular arbitrage with their cross rates for the dollar. For example, if the parity value of the British pound is $2.00 and the parity value of the French franc is $0.25, then triangular arbitrage would ensure that the exchange rate between the franc and the pound equals

$$(dollars/pound)/(dollars/franc) = (francs/pound)$$
$$(2.00) \ / \ (0.25) = 8.00$$

or eight francs per pound.

In turn, the willingness of countries to hold dollars as currency reserves was assured by the obligation of the U.S. to buy and sell gold from other central banks at a fixed price of $35 per ounce. If countries had temporary difficulty in maintaining reserves, they could borrow reserves from the IMF.

These IMF reserves were initially in gold and dollars. However, in the 1960s the IMF started issuing Special Drawing Rights (SDRs), which were assigned a value equal to the trade weighted average value of the major currencies. Countries could in turn use SDRs as reserves to buy and sell their currencies. The IMF would lend the reserves only if the country adopted the monetary and fiscal policies necessary to alleviate long-term pressure on the currency.

Because individual countries were responsible for maintaining the dollar parity rates of their currencies and their reserves could compensate only for temporary imbalances in supply and demand for their currency, they had to track their national balance of payments to keep track of the aggregate supply and demand for their currency. The balance of payments account was divided into three parts: the current account, which recorded supply and demand for the currency that resulted from international trade in goods and services; the capital account, which recorded supply and demand that resulted from international credit flows; and the reserve account, which recorded the government's purchase and sale of reserves to balance the supply and demand for the currency at its parity rate.

The Bretton Woods agreement successfully maintained a fixed exchange rate from the late 1940s to the early 1970s. Periodically, some countries had to adjust their parity rates with the dollar because it had become politically impossible to adopt the requisite fiscal and monetary policies.The system's collapse came in the early 1970s because of the unwillingness of the U.S. to adopt the fiscal and monetary policies necessary to maintain the price of gold. President Richard Nixon abandoned the convertibility of the dollar into gold at a fixed price and, one by one, the major industrial countries allowed their currency exchange rates to float.

The European Monetary System

Later in the 1970s, the European Economic Community (known as the Common Market) agreed to stabilize the exchange rates of member countries with respect to each other, while allowing the rates to float with respect to nonmember countries. This European Monetary System (EMS) is sometimes called the *snake*, because a graph of the dollar value of European currencies over time looks like a snake.

The currencies in the snake are tied together but float in relation to the dollar. Britain is the only major European nation that is not a member of the EMS; however, Britain may join as European economic integration accelerates after 1992.

In many ways, the EMS is like a regional Bretton Woods System. The role of the primary reserve currency is filled by the German mark. The role of gold and SDR reserves is filled by the *European Currency Unit* (ECUs), the value of which is equal to a trade weighted average of the currencies of the EMS countries. The ECU has received such widespread acceptance in Europe that many contracts and financial assets such as notes and bonds are denominated in ECUs rather than a particular currency. With the collapse of communism in Eastern Europe and Western European economic integration, the economic roles of Europe and the EMS are likely to grow rapidly. It is not inconceivable that the twenty-first century will witness the convertibility of such currencies as the Russian ruble or even the U.S. dollar and Japanese yen into ECUs at government-stabilized rates.

CHAPTER PERSPECTIVE

In order to avoid the economic instabilities associated with fluctuating exchange rates, governments often intervene in the foreign exchange market. Governments can attempt to influence exchange rates by fiat or by market intervention. A fiat can be either a law or a regulation that prohibits the exchange of currencies except at approved ratios. The result of setting exchange rates by fiat is often a black market or offshore trading where the excess supply or demand for a currency is met at illegal or unofficial exchange rates.

A more effective influence over exchange rates can be obtained by market intervention. Governments can influence supply and demand directly by purchasing or selling their own currency in exchange for reserves; they can influence supply and demand for their currency indirectly with appropriate fiscal and monetary policies that are designed to influence foreign trade and credit flows.

Government efforts to influence exchange rates are most effective when coordinated with other governments. The most effective system of international exchange rate coordination is currently the European Currency System. Adoption of an international treaty similar to the old Bretton Woods agreement is a clear possibility in the future.

Determining Forward Exchange Rates

INTRODUCTION AND MAIN POINTS

In Chapters 5 and 6, we examined factors that influence exchange rate movements. In this chapter we explore the factors that determine the forward exchange rate. While it is true that the forward exchange rate is a market price and therefore is determined by the supply and demand for forward exchange, factors such as trade, credit, and government intervention play only an indirect role in determining the forward rate.

The activities of two types of traders dominate the forward foreign exchange market: speculators, who buy and sell forward contracts based upon expectations of future spot rates, and arbitrageurs, who buy and sell forward contracts based upon differences in interest rates. This chapter focuses on the roles of these traders.

After studying the material in this chapter:

■ You will understand the determinants of the forward exchange rate.

■ You will be able to design simple speculative foreign exchange trading strategies.

■ You will be able to design simple interest rate arbitrage strategies.

■ You will understand the differences between the forward rate and future spot rates.

■ You will understand the risks associated with foreign exchange speculation.

■ You will understand the influence of interest rates on forward and spot exchange rates.

EXCHANGE RATE SPECULATION

If you expect the dollar value of a foreign currency to increase in the future, you may profit by buying the currency now at the lower price and holding it until it rises in value. If you expect the dollar value of the foreign currency to decline, then you would sell the currency for dollars and buy it back after the currency declined. However, you will not be interested in such buy-and-hold strategies unless the profits are large enough to compensate you for the interest forgone on other investments and the risk that the value of the currency may not rise.

One method of avoiding the cost of investing your funds in foreign currency is to contract to buy or sell the currency in the future at the forward exchange rate. For example, suppose you had information that led you to expect the value of the deutsche mark to be $0.60 in three months and knew that you could contract today with your bank to buy deutsche marks at the three month forward rate of $0.58. Three months later, if your expectation turned out to be correct, you could use your forward contract to buy the marks at $0.58, immediately sell them for $0.60 and earn a two-cent profit on each deutsche mark. If you expected the deutsche mark to sell for less than $0.58 in three months, you would contract to sell deutsche marks at the forward rate.

The profit obtained by speculating in the forward market would not have required any investment during the three months. However, you would have borne the risk that your expectation could turn out to be incorrect. You cannot be sure that you can buy or sell at the expected future spot rate. If you have contracted at the forward rate to sell a currency, then you must buy it at whatever the future spot rate turns out to be. Similarly, if you have contracted to buy a currency at the forward rate, you must sell it at the future spot rate. Since expectations of future spot rates often turn out to be wrong, due to the impact of unforeseen economic events, speculation in the forward exchange market is very risky.

The risk of speculating in the forward exchange market can be reduced by diversification. A professional currency speculator engages in thousands of forward exchange contracts. Although the speculator may often be wrong about the future value of the future spot rate, as long as the forecast of the direction of the change in the exchange rate is correct, a profit will result.

For example, suppose you have contracted to buy deutsche marks at the forward rate of $0.58. You will profit as long as the future spot rate turns out to be above $0.58; the higher the rate, the greater the profit. Over time, most of your unexpected losses from erroneous forecasts will be offset by unexpected profits from forecasts that are wrong about the future value of the spot rate but right about whether it is above or below the forward rate.

EFFECT OF SPECULATION ON FORWARD RATES

People who have either information or technical ability that enables them to forecast whether the future spot rate will turn out to be higher or lower than the forward rate can make substantial profits by buying or selling currency at the forward exchange rate. If the consensus of informed traders is that the forward rate is less than the expected future spot rate, then they will buy forward exchange. The increased demand will drive up the forward rate until speculators no longer feel that it is undervalued. If the consensus of speculators is that the forward rate is above the expected future spot rate, they will sell forward exchange and the increased supply will reduce the forward rate.

Since the supply and demand for foreign exchange that is induced by speculation drives the equilibrium forward exchange rate toward the market consensus of the expected future spot rate, it is often hypothesized that the best estimate of a currency's future value is the forward exchange rate. Financial economists call this hypothesis the *Unbiased Forward Rate Theory*.

This theory is hard to reject. Economists have used a variety of statistical tests to determine whether the forward rate is on average higher or lower than the subsequently observed spot rate. For example, we could record the one-month forward rate on the first day of each month from January 1980 to January 1991. The spot rates observed one month later from February 1980 to February 1991 would also be recorded. Statistical tests would then be used to determine if the average of the monthly differences between the forward rate and the subsequent spot rate are significantly different from zero. A finding that the differences equal zero on average would constitute support for the Unbiased Forward Rate Theory.

Even when the differences are on average equal to zero, the Unbiased Forward Rate Theory may not be valid. A second type of test records a time series of the differences between the forward rate and the subsequently observed spot rate and tests hypotheses that explain the behavior of the differences.

For example, suppose we suspected that the differences between the forward and the future spot rate would be positive when exports are increasing and negative when exports are decreasing. We could compare past data on export changes to the differences between the forward and the future spot rate. If our suspicion were confirmed by the data, we would reject the Unbiased Forward Rate Theory, since a knowledge of the forward rate and the change in exports would provide a better forecast of the future spot rate than just the forward rate alone.

Although many studies do support the Unbiased Forward Rate Theory, there are important exceptions to the hypothesis that the forward rate is the best estimate of the future spot rate. Opponents of the Unbiased Forward Rate Theory usually attribute evidence against the theory to either risk premiums or transaction costs that inhibit speculation. Transaction costs associated with bid/ask spreads reduce arbitrageurs' profits, while risks lead them to forgo small profits on minor differences between forward and expected future spot rates.

Economists who support the Unbiased Forward Rate Theory generally attribute statistical evidence against it to statistical errors. Financial managers and investors should probably not take either position but simply conclude that the forward rate is a reasonably good estimate of the future spot rate and view alternative estimates with caution.

INTEREST RATE ARBITRAGE
While speculation may offer potential profits to forward rate traders who are willing to take risks, interest rate arbitrage may offer risk-free profits to forward rate traders. Unfortunately, such risk-free profits are so small that only large financial institutions can engage in transactions of sufficient magnitude to make interest rate arbitrage attractive. Nevertheless, it is useful to understand the technique.

Borrowing and Lending Internationally
At any particular time, interest rates in one country are rarely equal to interest rates in other countries. For example, suppose you discover that you can borrow in Germany at six percent and lend in the U.S. at nine percent. The subscript "t" indicates the present time period and the subscript "t+1" indicates the next year. You could borrow one million deutsche marks at six percent for one year and convert them into dollars at the spot rate of 0.58 dollars per mark,

$$(DM_t)\ (\$/DM_t) = (\$_t)$$
$$(1,000,000)\ (0.58) = 580,000$$

which gives you $580,000. You lend the $580,000 for one year at nine percent:

$$(\$_t)\ (1 + r_{us}) = (\$_{t+1})$$
$$(580,000)\ (1 + 0.09) = 632,200$$

which gives you \$632,200 at the end of the year. However, you must use deutsche marks to pay off the loan, which has accrued interest in deutsche marks:

$$(DM_t) (1 + r_{ger}) = (DM_{t+1})$$
$$(1,000,000) (1 + 0.06) = 1,060,000$$

and now requires DM 1,060,000 to repay.

The problem with such a strategy is that the future spot rate for converting the dollars into deutsche marks at the end of the year is unknown at the time you borrow the marks and lend the dollars. Suppose the spot rate is \$0.59 per mark one year from now. Your \$632,200 would convert to

$$(\$_{t+1}) / (\$/DM_{t+1}) = (DM_{t+1})$$
$$(632,200) / (0.59) = 1,071,525.4$$

You would receive DM 1,071,525.4. After paying off the loan you would have a profit of DM 11,525.4 { = 1,071,525.4 − 1,060,000 }, which you could convert to dollars if you wished.

On the other hand, suppose the spot rate one year later turned out to be \$0.60 per deutsche mark. Your \$632,200 could be converted into

$$(632,200)/(0.60) = 1,053,666.7$$

Since you would receive DM 1,053,666.7, you would experience a loss of DM 6,333.3 after paying off the loan of DM 1,060,000.

You can avoid this uncertainy by contracting to buy deutsche marks at the forward rate for marks when you borrow the marks and lend the dollars. If after checking the forward rate you find that you would lose money by borrowing marks and lending dollars, then you can profit by borrowing dollars and lending marks.

For example, suppose the forward rate on the mark is \$0.60. As shown previously, you would lose DM 6,333.3 if you borrowed marks at six percent and lent dollars at nine percent. However, if you borrowed \$1,000,000, you could convert them at the current spot rate of \$0.58 per mark into

$$(\$_t) / (\$/DM_t) = (DM_t)$$
$$(1,000,000) / (0.58) = 1,724,137.93$$

You would have DM 1,724,137.93 and could lend them at six percent. At the end of the year you would have

$$(DM_t) (1 + r_{ger}) = (DM_{t+1})$$
$$(1,724,137.9) (1 + .06) = 1,827,586.21$$

You could convert these DM 1,827,586.21 at the forward rate of $0.60 into

$$(DM_{t+1}) (\$/DM_{t+1}) = (\$_{t+1})$$
$$(1,827,586.2) (0.60) = 1,096,551.72$$

Thus you would receive $1,096,551.72. You would need $1,090,000.00 to pay off the loan:

$$(\$_t) (1 + r_{us}) = (\$_{t+1})$$
$$(1,000,000) (1 + .09) = 1,090,000$$

and have a profit of $6,551.72.

Arbitrageurs do not care whether it is profitable to lend or profitable to borrow in their own currency. They are interested only in whether there is a potential profit. Once they know the interest rates and the spot and forward rates, they can easily determine the appropriate strategy.

Effect of Interest Rate Arbitrage on the Forward and Spot Rates
Interest rate arbitrage is risk-free because the foreign and domestic interest rates along with the current spot and forward exchange rates, are known at the time the transactions are initiated. The activities of arbitrageurs are reflected in the supply and demand for both forward and spot currency exchange, which in turn affects the forward and spot exchange rates.

Consider the interest rate arbitrage activity of a multinational bank that wishes to borrow dollars and lend in country X after converting the dollars into currency X and entering a forward exchange contract to reverse the exchange at the maturity of the loan. At maturity (t+1) the bank will owe (in dollars)

$$\$ (1 + r_{us})$$

It will have earned

$$X (1 + r_x)$$

units of currency X, which can be converted at the forward rate of $(\$/X)_{t+1}$ into a dollar amount

$$X (1 + r_x) (\$/X)_{t+1}$$

Since the amount of foreign currency (X) is equal to the amount of dollars borrowed ($) divided by the spot rate $(\$/X)_t$,

$$X = \$ / (\$/X)_t$$

the amount of dollars earned is

$$(\$ / (\$/X)_t) (1 + r_x) (\$/X)_{t+1}$$

The arbitrage profit to the bank is the amount of dollars earned less the amount of dollars owed:

$$\text{Profit} = \{(\$/(\$/X)_t) (1 + r_x) (\$/X)_{t+1} - \$ (1 + r_{us})\} \qquad [1]$$

In the market for spot exchange, the dollars are being exchanged for currency X, which creates additional demand for X and drives up its value in dollars $(\$/X)_t$. In the forward market, currency X is being exchanged for dollars, which creates an additional supply of currency X and drives down its value in dollars $(\$/X)_{t+1}$. The effect of both the increase in the spot rate $(\$/X)_t$ and the decrease in forward rate $(\$/X)_{t+1}$ is to reduce the earnings of the arbitrageur until the earnings are equal to the amount owed

$$(\$ / (\$/X)_t)(1 + r_x)(\$/X)_{t+1} = \$ (1 + r_{us}) \qquad [2]$$

and the potential profit is eliminated.

The impact of arbitrage activity on market prices eliminates the potential for more arbitrage profit. Readers can verify for themselves that if the bank found it profitable to borrow currency X and lend dollars, then the spot rate would be reduced and the forward rate would be increased until it was no longer profitable.

Equation [2] describes the equilibrium that results from arbitrage no matter which strategy is profitable at first. If we divide both sides of equation [2] by

$$\$ / (1 + r_x)$$

we find that the ratio of the forward rate to the spot rate is equal to the ratio of the return in the U.S. to the return in country X:

$$(\$/X)_{t+1} / (\$/X)_t = (1 + r_{us}) / (1 + r_x) \qquad [3]$$

Economists call the relationship between spot rates, forward rates, and interest rates expressed in equation [3] *interest rate parity*.

Interest rate parity is also often expressed in the following form:

$$(1 + f) = (1 + r_{us}) / (1 + r_x) \qquad [4]$$

where f is the forward premium or discount on currency X,

$$f = \{ (\$/X)_{t+1} - \$/X)_t \} / \$/X)_t$$

For example, if the interest rate in the U.S. is eight percent and the interest rate in Germany is six percent, then interest rate parity implies that the forward rate on the deutsche mark would be selling at a 1.89 percent premium, i.e.:

$$(1 + r_{us}) / (1 + r_{ger}) - 1 = f$$
$$(1 + .08) / (1 + .06) - 1 = 0.0189$$

The ratio of the forward rate to the spot rate on the deutsche mark would be 1.0189:

$$(1 + r_{us}) / (1 + r_{ger}) = \{ (\$/DM)_{t+1} / (\$/DM)_t \}$$
$$(1 + .08) / (1 + .06) = 1.0189$$

Using Interest Rate Parity to Quote Forward Rates

Banks rely on interest rate parity to make instant quotes on forward rates to their customers. Given the spot rate and interest rates in any two countries, banks can compute and quote a forward rate to their customers. If the customer buys a particular currency at the forward rate, the bank can then try to sell an equal amount of currency at a slightly higher price. If they are unable to sell the same amount of currency at the forward rate, the bank can hedge its risk by borrowing and lending appropriate amounts of the two currencies.

For example, suppose a bank is asked by an important American corporation for a forward rate contract to sell them 10 million deutsche marks in one year. The bank knows that current interest rates in Germany and the U.S. are six percent and eight percent, respectively, and that the current spot rate for the deutsche mark is $0.58. They use *interest rate parity* to compute the forward rate:

$$(1 + r_{us}) / (1 + r_{ger}) (\$/DM)_t = (\$/DM)_{t+1}$$
$$(1 + .08) / (1 + .06) (0.58) = 0.5909$$

They quote a forward rate of $0.60 per mark, which is slightly higher to allow for risk and profit. The bank would then try to eliminate its own exposure by buying 10 million deutsche marks at a forward rate of $0.59, which would give it a one-cent profit per mark. If the bank could not find a seller at that forward rate, it would use interest rate arbitrage to lock in a profit. This would require borrowing $5,471,698.10:

($/DM)t+1 / (1 + rger) ($/DM)t = $t
(10 million) /   (1 + .06) (0.58) = 5,471,698.10

It would convert the $5,471,698.10 into marks at the spot rate and invest the marks in Germany, which would give it DM 10 million:

$$\{(\$t) \ / \ (\$/DM)t\} \ (1 + rger) = (DMt+1)$$
$$\{(5,471,698.10) \ / \ (0.58)\} \quad (1+.06) = 10 \text{ million}$$

which would be sold to the American corporation for $6 million:

$$(DMt+1) \quad (\$/DM)t+1 = (\$t+1)$$
$$(10 \text{ million}) \quad (0.60) \quad = 6 \text{ million}$$

The bank would owe only $5,964,150.90:

$$(\$t) \qquad (1+ rus) \quad = (\$t+1)$$
$$(5,471,698.10) \ (1+.09) \quad = 5,964,150.90$$

on its loan. Hence, the bank would still earn a risk-free profit of $35,849.10 (= 6,000,000 − 5,964,150.90) on the total transaction.

Deviations from Interest Rate Parity

Almost all statistical studies support the theory of interest rate parity. Deviations from interest rate parity rarely exceed the size of transaction costs embodied in bid and ask spreads (see Chapter 3). Furthermore, many bankers report that they quote forward exchange rates to customers that are implied by interest rate parity in the absence of any observable market rates.

However, we frequently observe what appear to be large deviations from interest rate parity. These usually result from a failure to recognize an important underlying assumption regarding interest rate arbitrage.

Implicit in our presentation of interest rate arbitrage is the assumption that there is no possibility of default on international loans. We assume that a lender could be certain of receiving both the principal and the interest on the loan and that, if necessary, the lender could be sure of exchanging currencies at the forward or future spot rate. In addition, we assume that a lender could be sure that the borrower will pay both principal and interest.

In actual practice, none of these assumptions are completely justified. There is always some probability that one party to a contract may default. In addition sometimes governments unexpectedly intervene in markets and prevent the free flow and exchange of credit and currencies.

Tests of interest rate parity usually use data that most approximate the assumptions underlying risk-free interest rate arbitrage. Typically, the forward and spot rates used in these tests are taken from the interbank market, which records rates negotiated between the largest, most secure international banks. The interest rates usually observed are short-term Eurodeposit rates, which are the rates at which these large, secure multinational banks lend currency to one another for periods of between one and 12 months.

Interest rate parity is only a rough approximation of the relationship between forward rates and interest rates when the contracts are subject to substantial risk. The parties who bear the risk will incorporate varied and substantial risk premiums into their rates, which would inhibit arbitrage and create substantial deviations from parity.

CHAPTER PERSPECTIVE

Forward exchange rates are market prices and as such are determined by the supply and demand for forward exchange contracts. Supply and demand in turn are influenced by international credit movements and speculation. Speculation in forward rate contracts is limited by risks borne by speculators.

Interest rate arbitrage entails borrowing in one currency and lending in another. The risks of unexpected exchange rate changes can be avoided by locking in a future exchange rate with a forward exchange contract that matures at the same time as the loan and deposit. Since all risk is avoidable, arbitrage drives the forward rate to an equilibrium rate at which no additional profits are possible. Impediments to arbitrage can lead to divergences from interest rate parity.

Inflation Rates and Currency Values

INTRODUCTION AND MAIN POINTS

In Chapter 7, we examined the effect of interest rates and expections of future spot rates on forward rates. In this chapter we examine the effect of inflation rates, which influence interest rates, on future spot rates. We begin by analyzing the Law of One Price, which is based upon arbitrage in tradeable goods. The effect of inflation on the Law of One Price is then used to derive the concept of purchasing power parity, which relates inflation rates to future spot rates.

After studying the material in this chapter:

■ You will understand the arguments underlying the Law of One Price.

■ You will be able to recognize and exploit arbitrage opportunities in tradeable goods.

■ You will understand the impact of relative differences in inflation rates among different countries on future competitiveness.

■ You will understand the concept of purchasing power parity.

■ You will be able to analyze the long term influence of national price levels on the values of currencies.

■ You will understand the interactions of inflation rates and exchange rates on a company's competitiveness.

EXCHANGE RATES, INFLATION RATES, AND FOREIGN COMPETITION

Businesses face competition abroad when they try to export and domestically when they compete against imports. Exchange rates play a major role in defining the nature of both kinds of competition. If a business is profitably exporting its product, then a decrease in the value of the dollar will allow it to lower its foreign sales price and/or increase its profit margin on exports.

For example, if an American manufacturer can sell microchips in France for 60 francs each and the exchange rate of the dollar is six francs, then the company receives $10

$$(francs) / (francs/dollar) = (dollars)$$
$$(60) \quad / \quad (6) \quad = 10$$

for each chip. Assuming a cost of $9 per chip, the manufacturer makes a profit of $1 per chip.

If the value of the dollar decreases to five francs and the company maintains a price of 60 francs per chip in France, then the dollar revenue will increase to $12 per chip:

$$(francs) / (francs/dollar) = (dollars)$$
$$(60) \quad / \quad (5) \quad = 12$$

The profit margin per chip will triple, since the dollar cost will remain at $9 per chip.

The company can even reduce the price of the chips in France to 55 francs. It will still receive $11 per chip:

$$(francs) / (francs/dollar) = (dollars)$$
$$(55) \quad / \quad (5) \quad = (11)$$

The company's profit margin will double to $2 per chip, and the sales volume in France will increase as a result of the lower price.

The business would also do well in the U.S. against its French competitors. Suppose the French competitor had to receive 60 francs per chip in order to cover its costs. At an exchange rate of six francs per dollar, it could sell chips as low as $10 per chip. However, at an exchange rate of five francs per dollar, it would have to raise its price in the U.S. to $12 per chip in order to cover its costs:

$$(francs) / (francs/dollar) = (dollars)$$
$$(60) \quad / \quad (5) \quad = 12$$

In the absence of other changes, a decrease in the value of the dollar improves the competitive prospects of American businesses both at home and abroad. On the other hand, an increase in the value of the dollar has a negative effect on the competitive position of American businesses. However, exchange rates rarely change in the absence of other changes.

Exchange rate changes are almost always accompanied by the effects of inflation. Suppose that over the same period of time, the value of the dollar decreases from six to five francs, the U.S. experiences an inflation rate (p_{us}) of 30 percent. If all goods and services increase by 30 percent, then the manufacturer of the microchip would require $13 per chip in order to maintain the same income.

$$(\text{dollars}_t)(1 + p_{us}) = (\text{dollars}_{t+1})$$
$$(10) \quad (1 + .30) = 13$$

This would require the selling price of the chips to rise to 65 francs in France:

$$(\text{dollars}_{t+1})(\text{francs/dollar})_{t+1} = (\text{francs}_{t+1})$$
$$(13) \qquad (5) \qquad = 65$$

If inflation in France were only five percent, the American exporter would be at a disadvantage, since the French would expect to pay only 63 francs per chip:

$$(\text{francs}_t)(1 + p_{fra}) = (\text{francs}_{t+1})$$
$$(60) \quad (1 + .05) = 63$$

However, if France experienced an inflation rate (p_{fra}) of 10 percent then the price per chip could rise to 66 francs without incurring a competitive disadvantage:

$$(\text{francs}_t)(1 + p_{fra}) = (\text{francs}_{t+1})$$
$$(60) \quad (1 + .10) = 66$$

REAL EXCHANGE RATES

In order to determine the competitive impact of an exchange rate change, we must consider the combined effects of the new exchange rate and the inflation rate in the two countries. Financial economists use the real exchange rate $(FF/\$)_{real}$ to simplify this task:

$$(FF/\$)_{real} = (FF/\$)(1 + p_{us}) / (1 + p_{fra})$$

The real exchange rate can be thought of as the ratio of the real value of dollars $\{\$/(1 + p_{us})\}$ to the real value of francs $\{FF/(1 + p_{fra})\}$:

$$(FF/\$)_{real} = \{FF/(1 + p_{fra})\} / \{\$/(1 + p_{us})\}$$

To determine whether a combination of changes in exchange rates and inflation rates will make a product more or less competitive, you simply multiply the old dollar price by the real exchange rate. If the result is a franc price that is higher than the old franc price, then the product is less competitive; if it is lower than the old franc price, the product is more competitive.

For instance, in the previous example the value of the dollar fell to five francs and inflation was 30 percent and 10 percent in the U.S. and France, respectively. Multiplying the real exchange rate by the old dollar price of $10,

$$(\$) \ (\$/FF) \ (1 + p_{us}) \ / \ (1 + p_{fra}) = (FF)$$
$$(10) \ (5) \ (1 + .30) \ / \ (1 + .10) = 59.09$$

we see that the product is more competitive, since its real price falls to 59.09 francs. However, if the French inflation rate were only five percent, then

$$(\$) \ (\$/FF) \ (1 + p_{us}) \ / \ (1 + p_{fra}) = (FF)$$
$$(10) \ (5) \ (1 + .30) \ / \ (1 + .05) = 61.90$$

The product would be less competitive, since its real price would rise to 61.90 francs.

LAW OF ONE PRICE

In the previous examples, we explored the effect of exchange rate changes on the competitive position of the business. Implicit in the discussion was the assumption that if the real price of the company's exports rose, then the company would face difficulty but not extinction. The reason that businesses can survive a price disadvantage is that products are typically differentiated by other factors besides price.

For example, the price of a Mercedes-Benz may increase by 10 percent more than the price of a Cadillac due to a fall in the value of the dollar. But many people will continue to buy Mercedes rather than Cadillacs because the two types of cars are not perfect substitutes.

What happens when products *are* perfect substitutes? In such cases, price is the only factor that differentiates them, and an exchange rate change can eliminate the competition. In fact, arbitrageurs can operate profitably in markets for goods that are perfect substitutes.

Consider Arabian oil on board a tanker in the port of Rotterdam. Suppose the oil is owned by an American oil company and is for sale at the American price of $20 per barrel. Also, suppose that identical oil is on board a British tanker and is for sale at the British price of 12 pounds per barrel.

An arbitrageur would check the value of the pound in dollars. If the exchange rate is $1.80 per pound, then the arbitrageur would buy American oil for $20 per barrel and sell it in Britain for 12 pounds per barrel. For each barrel of oil, the arbitrageur would convert 12 pounds into $21.60:

$$(\text{pounds/barrel}) \, (\text{dollars/pound}) = (\text{dollars/barrel})$$
$$(12) \qquad\qquad (1.80) \qquad = 21.60$$

and earn a profit of $1.60 per barrel.

In the market for British oil, these actions would increase the supply and drive the price down. In the market for American oil the demand would increase and drive the price up. In the foreign exchange market, the arbitrageur would supply pounds for dollars and drive the price of the pound down. The price impacts in all three markets would have the effect of reducing the arbitrageur's profit until the pound price of oil times the exchange rate equaled the dollar price—eliminating all profit.

If the exchange rate is $1.60 per pound, the situation is reversed. Arbitrageurs will buy British oil for 12 pounds per barrel, sell it to Americans for $20 per barrel, and convert the $20 into 12.5 pounds for each barrel:

$$(\text{dollars/barrel}) \, / \, (\text{dollars/pound}) = (\text{pounds/barrel})$$
$$(20) \qquad / \qquad (1.6) \qquad = 12.5$$

This will increase the American price of oil and reduce the British price of oil. The exchange of dollars into pounds will increase the demand for pounds on the foreign exchange market, which will cause the pound's value in dollars to rise. As was true in the previous example, all of the price changes will have the effect of reducing the arbitrageur's profits until they are eliminated.

At equilibrium, when the arbitrageur's profits are eliminated, the price of oil will be the same in America and Britain when converted at the exchange rate. Economists call this condition the *Law of One Price*.

Algebraically, the Law of One Price states that the exchange rate must equal the ratio of the dollar price per item divided by the pound price per item:

$$(\text{dollars/pound}) = (\text{dollars/item}) / (\text{pounds/item})$$

This condition holds for any exchange rate. The value of the deutsche mark in yen equals the ratio of the Japanese price per item over the German price per item. In general, the exchange rate between currency A and currency B will be the ratio of the prices of item X in terms of the two currencies:

$$(A/B) = (A/X) / (B/X) \tag{1}$$

The Law of One Price never holds precisely for all goods and services because of transactions costs, time delays, and trade restrictions that inhibit arbitrage. The best example of the Law of One Price is gold, for which the restrictions on arbitrage constitute a very small proportion of its value. For goods that are not perfect substitutes and services that are difficult to import and export, the Law of One Price is a poor description. Nevertheless, on average the Law of One Price does seem to hold.

PURCHASING POWER PARITY

We now consider the impact of inflation on arbitrage in goods that are perfect substitutes. For simplicity, assume that all goods and services in a particular country increase in price at the same rate of inflation. One period from now the Law of One Price will still hold. Hence, at time period t,

$$(A/B)_t = (A/X)_t / (B/X)_t \tag{2}$$

and one period later, at t+1,

$$(A/B)_{t+1} = (A/X)_{t+1} / (B/X)_{t+1} \tag{3}$$

In the previous sections we saw that the price next period is simply the price in the preceding period times one plus the inflation rate, so

$$(A/X)_{t+1} = (A/X)_t (1 + p_a) \tag{4}$$

and

$$(B/X)_{t+1} = (B/X)_t (1 + p_b) \tag{5}$$

where p_a and p_b are the rates of inflation for currency a and b, respectively. Substituting equations [4] and [5] into equation [3], we get an equation for the future value of the exchange rate in terms of current prices of item X and the two rates of inflation:

$$(A/B)_{t+1} = (A/X)_t (1 + p_a) / (B / X)_t (1 + p_b) \qquad [6]$$

Consider the ratio of the future exchange rate and the current exchange rate. We can obtain an equation for this ratio by simply dividing equation [6] by equation [4]:

$$(A/B)_{t+1}/(A/B)_t = \{(A/X)_t(1+p_a)/(B/X)_t(1+p_b)\}/\{(A/X)_t/(B/X)_t\}$$

Canceling the prices of item X reduces this equation to

$$(A/B)_{t+1}/(A/B)_t = (1+p_a) / (1+p_b) \qquad [7]$$

which economists call *purchasing power parity*.

Purchasing power parity is generally expressed in terms of the percentage change in the exchange rate over period t:

$$e_t = \{(A/B)_{t+1} - (A/B)_t\} / (A/B)_t \qquad [8]$$

For example, suppose an exchange rate (A/B) increased from 10 to 11 in one year. The percentage change (e_t) would be 10 percent $\{= (11- 10)/10\}$. Equation [8] can also be expressed as

$$(1+e_t) = \{(A/B)_{t+1} / (A/B)_t\} \qquad [9]$$

Substituting equation [9] into equation [7] permits us to express purchasing power parity as an equation relating the percentage change in the exchange rate between currency a and currency b to the inflation rates for the two currencies:

$$(1 + e_t) = (1 + p_a) / (1 + p_b) \qquad [10]$$

Purchasing power parity allows us to forecast future changes in the exchange rate given knowledge of current inflation rates. For example, suppose the current inflation rate in the U.S. is six percent and the current inflation rate in Britain is nine percent. We would expect the value of the pound to decrease by slightly more than 2.75 percent, since

$$(1 - 0.0275) = (1 + .06) / (1 + .09)$$

An important implication of purchasing power parity is that the competitive position of a business will not change when the exchange rate changes. The reason is that the effect of the change in the exchange rate is perfectly offset by changes in costs and revenues caused by the different inflation rates. For example, suppose an American mill can produce a sheet of plywood for $3 and sell it in the U.S. for $4, making a profit of $1 per sheet. If the current exchange rate is $2.00 per pound, it can make the same profit by selling it in Britain for two pounds per sheet:

$$(\text{dollars}) \ / \ (\text{dollars/pound}) = (\text{pounds})$$
$$(4) \quad / \quad (2) \quad = (2)$$

If over the next year, the inflation rate in the U.S. increases the selling price by six percent, then the plywood will have to be sold for $4.24 per sheet, as follows:

$$(\text{dollars/sheet})_t \ (1 + p_{us}) = (\text{dollars/sheet})_{t+1}$$
$$(4) \qquad (1 + .06) = 4.24$$

If the value of the pound decreases by 2.75 percent, as described in the preceding example, then the exchange rate in one year will be $1.945 per pound:

$$(\text{dollars/pound})_t \ (1 + e) \ = (\text{dollars/pound})_{t+1}$$
$$(2.00) \quad (1 - .0275) = 1.945$$

At the lower value of the pound, the mill will have to charge 2.18 pounds per sheet of plywood:

$$(\text{dollars}) \ / \ (\text{dollars/pound}) = (\text{pounds})$$
$$(4.24) \quad / \quad (1.945) \quad = 2.18$$

Since in our example inflation in Britain is nine percent, the price of competing plywood will also have risen to 2.18 pounds per sheet of plywood:

$$(\text{pounds})_t \ (1 + p_{br}) = (\text{pounds})_{t+1}$$
$$(2) \quad (1 + .09) = 2.18$$

Hence, when purchasing power parity holds, the competitive position of the company is unchanged.

Deviations from Purchasing Power Parity

To what extent does purchasing power parity hold? The question is very difficult to answer because we cannot measure inflation rates very well. Economists agree that inflation is a reduction in the purchasing power of money. But they disagree about how to measure it. The difficulty results from trying to define purchasing power when different consumers purchase so many different goods and services.

Consider an economy in which there is only one good consumed, for example, milk. We would have no problem measuring inflation. It would simply be the percentage change in the price of milk. Now suppose a second good is introduced, for example, honey. How would we measure inflation?

We could take the percentage change in the price of milk and the percentage change in the price of honey and average the two. But this would not measure the change in purchasing power for an individual who chooses to consume very little honey and the change in purchasing power for an individual who chooses to consume a lot of honey. In fact the change in purchasing power depends upon what is consumed. The matter gets even more complex if the amounts of product consumed change as a result of price changes.

In a modern economy with millions of different consumers, products, and services, there is simply no right way to measure inflation. Hence, economists have developed many different types of averages of price changes on selected groups of products and services, including the Gross National Product (GNP) deflator, the Producer Price Index, different types of consumer price indexes, and wholesale price indexes.

Many different types of inflation measures have been used to test purchasing power parity, and the results vary accordingly. Some tests have used a special inflation rate that measures price changes for internationally traded goods only. No one concludes that purchasing power parity is an accurate description of the relationship between exchange rates and inflation rates. However, most concede that it is a fair description of the average relationship over extended periods of time.

In the short run, purchasing power parity almost never holds, and most economists would object to its use as a description of short-term relationships between inflation rates and exchange rates. However, some economists have argued that, since no one has successfully explained the behavior of the deviations from purchasing power parity, we can conclude that it is an unbiased predictor of exchange rate changes.

Even economists who do not reject purchasing power parity caution against ignoring the possibility of changes in the real values of individual foreign products. For a given average inflation rate, there are always large variations in relative prices. For example, the inflation rate may increase moderately while prices for energy products decline sharply and prices for medical services increase sharply. In the case of particular industries, one should be very careful about assuming that purchasing power parity holds, even in the long run.

CHAPTER PERSPECTIVE

Just as trade influences the exchange rate, exchange rates influence trade by changing the competitive positions of businesses both at home and abroad. In order to analyze the effect of exchange rate changes on a company's competitive position, we must also recognize the effect of both foreign and domestic inflation. The concept of a real exchange rate, which is simply an inflation-adjusted exchange rate, can be used to simplify the analysis of the company's competitive position.

Arbitrageurs can trade in goods that are perfect substitutes, such as oil or gold. The effect of arbitrage in goods on the equilibrium exchange rate is described by the Law of One Price.

Purchasing power parity describes the effect of inflation on exchange rates that are determined by the Law of One Price. An important implication of purchasing power parity is that the competitive position of the company is unchanged by the exchange rate when it holds. Unfortunately, purchasing power parity holds only in the long run, and its accuracy depends heavily on the particular measure of inflation that is used.

International Capital Market Equilibrium

INTRODUCTION AND MAIN POINTS

In the preceding two chapters, we encountered the theories of unbiased forward rates, interest rate parity, and purchasing power parity. These theories constitute three parts of what economists call the International Parity Conditions. In this chapter, we build upon these concepts to develop the remaining two International Parity Conditions, which are called the International Fisher Effect and the Global Fisher Effect.

The International Parity Conditions are interactive and dependent on one another. When viewed together, they provide a complete description of international capital market equilibrium. An understanding of this equilibrium is essential to anyone who operates in our global economy, including investors, business managers, and government economic policymakers.

After studying the material in this chapter:

■ You will understand the relationship between interest rates and future exchange rate changes.

■ You will be able to design risky interest rate arbitrage strategies and evaluate potential gains and losses.

■ You will understand and be able to estimate the differences between real and nominal rates of return.

■ You will understand the relationship between real interest rates in different countries and recognize factors that may cause them to differ.

■ You will understand and be able to calculate continuously compounded rates of return.

■ You will be able to use continuous compounding to simplify explanations of the International Parity Conditions.

THE INTERNATIONAL FISHER EFFECT

The Fisher Effect is a theory attributed to an early-twentieth-century economist, Irving Fisher, who argued that domestic interest rates would reflect anticipated levels of inflation. He is also recognized for a theory that relates expected changes in the exchange rate to differences in interest rates between countries. This theory is now known as the *International Fisher Effect*.

The International Fisher Effect is the subject of the first part of this chapter. It can hold either as a result of the interaction of unbiased forward rates and interest rate parity or as a result of a risky form of interest rate arbitrage. We explore the implications of both mechanisms.

Later in this chapter, we explore the *Global Fisher Effect*, which relates differences in interest rates among countries to differences in their expected inflation rates. Although somewhat confusing at first, these three types of Fisher effects provide the basis for understanding international capital market equilibrium.

Unbiased Forward Rates and Interest Rate Parity

We begin the study of the International Fisher Effect by reviewing the theories of unbiased forward rates and interest rate parity. In Chapter 7 we learned about interest rate parity, which shows that the ratio of a currency's forward rate $F\{(A/B)_{t+1}\}$ to its spot rate $(A/B)_t$ is a function of the interest rates in the respective countries:

$$F\{(A/B)_{t+1}\} / (A/B)_t = (1 + r_a) / (1 + r_b) \qquad [1]$$

where $F\{\ \}$ is used to indicate the forward contract rate for the currency exchange rate enclosed in the parentheses. We also learned about the Unbiased Forward Rate Theory, which shows that the forward rate equals the expected future spot rate:

$$F\{(A/B)_{t+1}\} = E\{(A/B)_{t+1}\} \qquad [2]$$

where $E\{\ \}$ is used to indicate the expected value of the variable enclosed by the parentheses.

If we divide both sides of equation [2] by $(A/B)_t$, then the Unbiased Forward Rate Theory can be expressed as ratios of the spot rate:

$$F\{(A/B)_{t+1}\} / (A/B)_t = E\{(A/B)_{t+1}\} / (A/B)_t \qquad [3]$$

If we assume that both interest rate parity and the Unbiased Forward Rate Theory hold true, then we can substitute equation [3] into equation [1] and obtain the following equation:

$$E\{(A/B)_{t+1}\} / (A/B)_t = (1 + r_a) / (1 + r_b) \qquad [4]$$

The relationship expressed in equation [4] is known as the *International Fisher Effect*, referred to by some economists as the "Fisher Open Condition" in contrast to the "Fisher Closed Condition," which refers to interest rate parity.

Since the ratio of the expected future spot rate to the current spot rate can be expressed as one plus the expected percentage change in the spot rate $(E\{e\})$, i.e.,

$$E\{e\}=\{E[\ (A/B)_{t+1}] - (A/B)_t\}/(A/B)_t$$

Hence,

$$(1 + E\{e\})=(1+ r_a)/(1 + r_b) \qquad [5]$$

In this more common form, the International Fisher Effect states that the expected percentage change in the exchange rate is a function of the different interest rates in the two countries. For example, if the Unbiased Forward Rate Theory and interest rate parity hold in the U.S. and Japan, where the interest rates are eight percent and four percent, respectively, we would expect the value of the yen to increase by 3.85 percent over the next year:

$$(1+ r_{us}) \ / \ (1 + r_{jap}) - \ 1 = E\{e\}$$
$$(1 + .08) \ / \ (1 + .04) - \ 1 = 0.0385$$

Although it is extremely unlikely that the exchange rate would actually increase by this much, it is our best estimate. The estimate is just as likely to be too low as it is to be too high.

Risky Arbitrage

If the International Fisher Effect does not hold, then arbitrageurs can expect to earn substantial profits by borrowing and lending in different countries. Suppose that the current spot rate for the Japanese yen is $0.0070. As shown in the previous section, if the interest rates in Japan and the U.S. are eight percent and nine percent, respectively, the International Fisher Effect would imply an increase of 3.85 percent in the value of the yen.

However, suppose an arbitrageur is confident that the yen will actually rise by four percent. How could a profit be obtained if the arbitrageur is correct? If the arbitrageur is correct, the future spot rate will turn out to be $0.00728 in one year:

$$(\$/y)_t (1+ e) = (\$/y)_{t+1}$$
$$(00700)(1+.04) = .00728$$

If the arbitrageurs borrow $1 million, in one year they will owe $1,080,000:

$$(\$_t)(1 + r_{us}) = (\$_{t+1})$$
$$(1 \text{ million})(1 + .09) = 1,080,000$$

If they take the $1 million and convert it to yen at the current spot rate, they will have 142,857,143 yen:

$$(\$_t) \quad / \quad (\$/¥)_t = (¥_t)$$
$$(1 \text{ million}) / (.007) = 142,857,143$$

If they lend the yen in Japan at four percent, they will have 148,571,429 yen in one year:

$$(¥_t)(1 + r_{jap}) = (¥_{t+1})$$
$$(142,857,143)(1 + .04) = 148,571,429$$

After converting the yen into dollars at the future spot rate, they will have $1,081,600:

$$(¥_{t+1})(\$/¥)_{t+1} = (\$_{t+1})$$
$$(148,571,429)(.00728) = 1,081,600$$

which will give them a profit of $1600 in one year. If arbitrageurs expect the value of the yen to increase by less than 3.85 percent, then they can profit by borrowing in Japan and lending in the U.S.

We should remember, however, that these arbitrage profits are earned only if the future spot rate actually turns out to be $.00728. If the value of the yen turns out to be less, they will earn less; if the future spot rate turns out to be higher, they will earn more. If the yen increases by less than 3.85 percent, then they will actually lose. The International Fisher Effect implies that 3.85 percent is the expected rate of increase and that 50 percent of the time it will be more and 50 percent of the time it will be less. This type of speculation should be avoided by investors and companies that cannot bear the risk.

Note from the example that when the rate of change in the spot rate implied by the International Fisher Effect is less than the arbitrageurs' expected rate of change, they demand yen at the spot rate and supply yen at the future spot rate. The extra demand for yen in the spot market increases its value, while the extra supply of yen in the future spot market decreases its value. The combined effect is to reduce the expected change in the value of yen until it conforms to the rate of change implied by the International Fisher Effect. The potential for arbitrage profit is eliminated.

We have shown that the combination of unbiased forward rates and interest rate parity implies that the International Fisher Effect holds. But it is also true that the condition of any two of these parity conditions implies that the third holds. For example, the International Fisher Effect and interest rate parity imply that forward rates are unbiased. Unbiased forward rates and the International Fisher Effect imply interest rate parity. Hence, confidence in the mechanisms that ensure that any two of the parity conditions hold promotes confidence that the remaining parity condition also holds.

THE GLOBAL FISHER EFFECT

We now turn our attention to the *Global Fisher Effect* that relates differences among interest rates in different countries to differences in their expected inflation rates. Before developing the Global Fisher Effect, we clarify the meaning of the *Fisher Effect* that relates interest rates to anticipated inflation rates in the domestic economy. We then show how the Global Fisher Effect is implied by the *International Fisher Effect* and purchasing power parity.

Real Versus Nominal Rates of Return

The real interest rate (i) is the rate of return that borrowers would pay and lenders would receive in the absence of inflation. In the presence of inflation, borrowers will pay and lenders will receive currency that is worth less than it was when it was lent or borrowed. If inflation is expected, lenders will insist on, and borrowers will agree to, a rate of return that compensates for the effect of inflation.

For example, if you expect a positive inflation rate $\{E(p)\}$ and lend money, you will demand that the borrower repay the loan amount (\$), plus a real rate of return (i \$), plus compensation for the inflated value of the loan amount $\{E(p)\ \$\}$, plus compensation for the inflated value of the real interest earned $\{E(p)\ i\ \$\}$:

$$\$ + i\ \$ + E(*p)\ \$ + E(p)\ i\ \$$$

which, after factoring out \$, equals

$$\$\ (1 + i + E(p) + E(p)\ i) = \$\ (1 + i)(1 + E(p))$$

In order to earn this return, you must charge a nominal interest rate (r) that will provide principal ($) plus interest (r $)

$$\$ + r\$ = \$ (1 + r)$$

that is equivalent to

$$\$ (1 + r) = \$ (1 + i) (1 + E(p)) \qquad [6]$$

Dividing both sides of equation [6] by ($), we obtain an equation

$$(1 + r) = (1 + i) (1 + E(p)) \qquad [7]$$

that relates the nominal interest rate (r) to the real interest rate (i) and the expected rate of inflation (E(p)). Economists call this relationship the *Fisher Effect*.

The Fisher Effect is frequently used in finance. For example, if you require a real rate of return of six percent and expect inflation to be 10 percent, then you will require a nominal rate of 16.6 percent,

$$(1 + i) \quad (1 + E(p)) - 1 = r$$
$$(1 + .06) \quad (1 + .10) - 1 \ = .166$$

On the other hand, if you are earning a nominal return of 15 percent and expect eight percent inflation, you would expect a real return of 6.48 percent:

$$(1 + r) \quad /(1 + E(p)) - 1 = i$$
$$(1 + .15) \ / \ (1 + .08) - 1 \ = .0648$$

Remember, you may not actually earn a real return of 6.48 percent. You can only expect it. If the actual inflation rate turns out to be higher, then the real return will be less. And if the actual inflation rate turns out to be lower, then the real return will be more.

Purchasing Power Parity and the International Fisher Effect

The *Fisher Effect* relates interest rates to inflation rates, while purchasing power parity and the *International Fisher Effect* relate inflation rates and interest rates to changes in exchange rates. The combined effect of these parity conditions implies the *Global Fisher Effect*. We have seen in Chapter 7 that purchasing power parity can be expressed algebraically as

$$(1 + e) = (1 + p_a)/(1 + p_b)$$

If we specify the expected rates of inflation $\{E(p)\}$, we can express purchasing power parity in terms of expected changes in the spot rate:

$$(1 + E(e)) = (1 + E(p_a)) / (1 + E(p_b))\qquad[8]$$

Substituting equation [5] for the International Fisher Effect into equation [8], we obtain

$$(1 + r_a) / (1 + r_b) = (1 + E(p_a)) / (1 + E(p_b))\qquad[9]$$

We call the relationship expressed in equation [9] the *Global Fisher Effect*. It relates relative interest rates to relative expected inflation rates.

A simpler explanation of the Global Fisher Effect relies upon the Fisher Effect. If we rearrange terms in equation [7], we can get

$$(1 + i) = (1 + r)/(1 + E(p))\qquad[10]$$

Rearranging terms in equation [9], we can get

$$(1 + r_a) / (1 + E(p_a)) = (1 + r_b) / (1 + E(p_b))\qquad[11]$$

Substituting equation [10] into [11] reveals that the Global Fisher Effect implies that expected real rates of return are the same in any two (all) countries for which purchasing power parity and the International Fisher Effect hold.

$$i_a = i_b\qquad[12]$$

Unlike the International Fisher Effect, which relates differences in national interest rates to expected changes in the value of the exchange rate, the Global Fisher Effect relates them directly to differences in expected inflation rates. Aside from this, however, the two Fisher Effects are really saying the same thing.

Differences in inflation rates are due to expectations about changes in the relative value of the underlying currencies. The International Fisher Effect measures the change in the relative value of the currencies by measuring the change in the exchange rate, while the Global Fisher Effect measures the change in the relative value of the currencies by measuring relative inflation rates. As long as the international parity conditions are not violated, the economic policies of individual nations can only influence inflation rates and nominal interest rates.

For example, if purchasing power parity and the International Fisher Effect are expected to hold for the U.S., Japan, Germany, France, and Britain, then the real rate of interest in these countries is the same regardless of differences in monetary policy, fiscal policy, national savings rates, economic growth, or a host of other factors that are commonly alleged to affect the real rate of interest.

If the Global Fisher Effect holds, we must learn to view our national capital markets as but a part of a truly global economic village. If nations wish to influence real rates of return independently, they must rely on policies such as taxes, price controls, rationing, and capital restrictions, that will separate them from world markets. As events in recent years demonstrate, even former Communist Bloc countries find this to be too high a price for independence from the market.

ANOTHER VIEW OF THE INTERNATIONAL PARITY CONDITIONS

Although the five international parity conditions are easy to work with mathematically, their complexity makes them difficult to work with intuitively or to explain to others. These difficulties can be eliminated by expressing the parity conditions in terms of continuously compounded rates of change.

The next section introduces and explains the mathematics of continuous compounding. This math is then used in the following section to simplify the parity conditions. Readers who are uninterested in the mathematics of continuous compounding can skip to the simplified summary of the parity conditions on page 90. The simplified equations can still serve as rough approximations even though they are not entirely accurate unless continuously compounded rates are used.

Continuous Compounding

We begin by defining x (note the use of a lower-case letter) as a rate of change over time in X (note the use of an upper-case letter). Hence,

$$x = (X_{t+1} - X_t) / X_t \qquad [13]$$

and

$$x = X_{t+1} / X_t - 1 \qquad [14]$$

When something grows at rate (x), we obtain its value next period by multiplying it by one plus the rate of change, which is called *compounding*.

$$X_{t+1} = X_t (1 + x)$$ [15]

These equations are familiar since interest rates, inflation rates, and exchange rate changes are all rates of change and function the same way. Up to this point, we have always assumed that t and t+1 referred to years, which is called annual compounding. If the periods between changes are less than one year, we divide the rate of change (x) by the number of periods per year (m) to get the rate of change per period (x/m).

If we make the period of time between changes infinitely small, called continous compounding, the growth is determined by multiplying X by (e^x)

$$X_{t+1} = X_t e^x$$ [16]

The mathematical term (e) is Euler's Constant, which is similar in some ways to the constant pi but has an approximate value of 2.71828. Most calculators have a function labeled (e^x). If you enter the value (1) into the calculator and press the (e^x) function key, the calculator will return the value 2.71828, since any number raised to the first power is unchanged (specifically, $e^1 = e$).

For example, the value of $1000 in savings after compounding annually at a 10 percent interest rate is $1100:

$$\$_t(1 + r) = \$_{t+1}$$
$$(1000) (1 + .10) = 1100$$

If the interest is compounded continuously, the value is $1105.17:

$$\$_t(e^r) = \$_{t+1}$$
$$(1000) e^{(10)} = 1105.17$$

The extra $5.17 is the result of earning more interest on interest as the compounding interval is reduced and interest is paid more frequently.

Annual rates of change (x^*) can be converted into continuous rates of change (x) by using the natural log function key (lnx) on a calculator. Comparing equations [15] and [16], we see that

$$(1 + x^*) = e^x$$ [17]

From the definition of a natural log, it is known that

$$\ln (e^x) = x$$ [18]

Substituting equation [17] into [18] shows us how to convert an annual rate of change (x^*) into a continuous rate of change (x):

$$\ln(1 + x^*) = x \qquad [19]$$

For example, an annual inflation rate of 10 percent is equivalent to a continuously compounded rate of 9.53 percent:

$$\ln(1 + .10) = .0953$$

An annual interest rate of eight percent is equivalent to a continuously compounded rate of 7.7 percent:

$$\ln(1 + .08) = .0770$$

An increase of 12 percent per year in the exchange rate is equivalent to a continuously compounded rate of change of 11.33 percent:

$$\ln(1 + .12) = .1133$$

Equation [17] shows how continuous rates can be converted into annual rates:

$$e^x - 1 = x^* \qquad [20]$$

For example, a continuous interest rate of 10 percent is equivalent to an annual rate of 10.52 percent:

$$e^{(10)} - 1 = .1052$$

A continuous inflation rate of six percent is equivalent to an annual inflation rate of 6.18 percent:

$$e^{(.06)} - 1 = .0618$$

There are also two algebraic rules about natural logs that are useful when analyzing the parity conditions. The natural log of a product equals the sum of the natural logs. For example,

$$\ln\{(1 + x)(1 + y)\} = \ln(1 + x) + \ln(1 + y) \qquad [21]$$

The natural log of a ratio equals the natural log of the numerator minus the natural log of the denominator. For example,

$$\ln\{(1 + x)/(1 + y)\} = \ln(1 + x) - \ln(1 + y) \qquad [22]$$

THE INTERNATIONAL PARITY CONDITIONS

Consider interest rate parity as it is expressed in annual rates of return (see Chapter 7):

$$(1+f^*) = (1 + r_a^*)/(1 + r_b^*)$$

where f^* is the forward exchange rate premium and the interest rates in countries a and b are denoted r_a^* and r_b^*, respectively. We can take the natural logs of this expression

$$f = r_a - r_b \qquad [23]$$

and obtain an equation for interest rate parity expressed in continuous rates of return. Equation [23] is a much simpler relation. It tells us that the difference in interest rates between two countries equals the forward premium or discount on the currency.

For example, if interest rates are six percent in Japan and nine percent in the United States, the forward rate on the Japanese yen will be selling at a three percent premium to the spot rate. Much of what we read in the popular press is based upon this form of interest rate parity.

While this form of interest rate parity is simple and easy to compute, it can be misleading if we fail to recall or are not familiar with the mathematics of continuous compounding. For example, a three percent continuously compounded premium on the spot rate is equivalent to a 3.05 percent annual rate of change:

$$e^f - 1 = f^*$$
$$e^{(.03)} - 1 = .0305$$

The annual interest rates are 9.42 percent and 6.18 percent in the U.S. and Japan, respectively:

$$e^r - 1 = r^*$$
$$e^{(.06)} - 1 = .0618$$
$$e^{(.09)} - 1 = .0942$$

Purchasing power parity can be expressed in the form of continuous rates:

$$E\{ e \} = E\{ p_a \} - E\{ p_b \} \qquad [24]$$

which attributes the expected change in the spot rate to the difference in the expected inflation rates. However, we must remember to convert the inflation rates reported in the press as annual rates into continuously compounded rates.

For example, an annual rate of inflation in the U.S. of seven percent should be converted into a continuous rate of 6.77 percent,

$$\ln(1 + p^*_{us}) = p_{us}$$
$$\ln(1 + .07) = (.0677)$$

An annual rate of inflation in Japan of five percent should be converted to a continuous rate of 4.88 percent.

$$\ln(1 + p^*_{jap}) = p_{jap}$$
$$\ln(1 + .05) = (.0488)$$

The expected continuous rate of change in value of the yen is the difference in the inflation rates, 1.89 percent ($= .0677 - .0488$), but this translates into an annual increase of 1.91 percent:

$$E(e) - 1 = E\{e^*\}$$
$$e^{(.0189)} - 1 = (.0191)$$

The remaining parity conditions can also be expressed in continous rates.

In summary, the International Parity Conditions expressed in continously compounded rates are:

Unbiased Forward Rates
$$f = E\{e\}$$

Interest Rate Parity
$$f = r_a - r_b$$

Purchasing Power Parity
$$E\{e\} = E\{p_a - E\{p_b\}$$

International Fisher Effect
$$E\{e\} = ra - rb$$

Global Fisher Effect
$$r_a - E\{p_a\} = r_b - E\{p_b\}$$

CHAPTER PERSPECTIVE

The International Parity Conditions constitute an interdependent description of world capital market equilibrium. If forward rates are unbiased and interest rate parity holds in two countries, then we can conclude that the International Fisher Effect also holds. Any two of these implies the third. If the International Fisher Effect and purchasing power parity hold for two countries, then we can conclude that the Global Fisher Effect also holds.

Interest rates and inflation rates, along with spot rates and forward rates, cannot change independently of one another. You must recognize the effects of one upon the other as embodied in the parity conditions if you are to make rational forecasts and decisions in a global capital market. The use of continuously compounded rates of change makes possible a very useful simplification of the parity conditions. However, you cannot ignore the mathematics of continuous time when making forecasts and decisions.

Forecasting and the Efficiency of International Markets

CHAPTER 10

INTRODUCTION AND MAIN POINTS

Most of international finance revolves around the difficulties that must be faced when transacting business in multiple currencies. Success in most areas of international finance requires an in-depth understanding of what determines exchange rates and why they change over time. Chapter 9 completed the presentation of most of what financial economists can agree upon about exchange rates and their movement over time. Much of the remainder of this book presents applications of this knowledge.

This chapter explores the ability of exchange rate speculators to profit from an understanding of exchange rate determination. We begin by reviewing speculative trading strategies. The concept of an efficient foreign exchange market is introduced in order to assess the degree of difficulty involved in currency speculation. The international parity conditions are then used to develop some simple speculative models. The chapter concludes by exploring some alternative strategies.

After studying the material in this chapter:
▬ You will understand the basic mechanisms of currency speculation.
▬ You will understand the concept of market efficiency as it applies to currency speculation.
▬ You will be able to use the international parity conditions to develop forecasts of future exchange rates.
▬ You will be introduced to methods of developing alternative exchange rate forecasting models.
▬ You will learn how to evaluate the performance of forecasting models using past exchange rate series.

PROFITING FROM EXCHANGE RATE FORECASTS

Making a profit on exchange rate forecasts basically is the same as making a profit in any investment. You try to buy at a low price and sell at a high price. In Chapter 7 we saw how speculators operated in the forward exchange market. If their forecast of the future spot rate was higher than the forward rate, they bought currency (low) at the forward rate and then sold it (high) at the future spot rate when the forward contract matured. If their forecast was correct, they made money. They even made money if the forecast was wrong, as long as the spot rate turned out to be higher than the forward rate. If their forecasted spot rate was lower than the forward rate, they simply reversed their strategy.

For reasons explained in Chapter 3, many potential currency speculators are not able to trade in the forward market. These individuals and companies can still profit from their forecasts of currency values by trading in the futures market. The buy-low, sell-high strategy is still used. If the forecasted future spot rate is below the futures price, sell the futures contract short. As the spot rate falls, the futures price will also fall. Each day the futures exchange marks the contract to market and deposits the profit into the speculator's account. When the futures price falls, as much as the speculator believes it will, he simply buys an identical contract. That evening the futures exchange will simply cancel the short and long positions. The speculator is left with all his profits and no remaining contract.

As is the case when speculating in the forward market, your forecast does not have to be accurate for you to profit. If you forecast a future spot rate below the futures price, you sell the futures contract and profit unless the futures price goes up or stays the same. Conversely, if you forecast a future spot rate above the futures price, you buy the futures contract and profit unless its price goes down or stays the same.

The problem with speculating in the forward or futures market is that you risk large losses if the exchange rate moves in a direction opposite to your forecast. Speculators can limit their loss potential by trading in currency options; however, they must pay the premium on the option in order to do so.

For example, suppose you forecast a future spot rate that is above the exercise price of a call option. You can buy the call option. If the future spot rate turns out to be equal to, or less than, the exercise price, you can discard the option and limit your loss to what you paid for the option. If the future spot rate exceeds the exercise price, the value of the option will rise and you can sell it at the higher price to a specialist who will profit from exercising it. If you forecast a future spot rate below the exercise price of a put option, you buy the put. Your loss is limited to the price you paid for the option, while your profit is limited only by how far the spot rate can fall.

EFFICIENCY OF THE FOREIGN EXCHANGE MARKET

Strategies for profiting from currency speculation are not too complex even for modest investors. How well can a speculator expect to perform? This question is probably best addressed by discussing the efficiency of the foreign exchange market.

Financial economists define an *efficient market* as one in which prices accurately reflect all available information. Put more simply, in an efficient market the price is right, not too high and not too low. An *efficient foreign exchange market* is one in which exchange rates are not too high and not too low.

An implication of an efficient foreign exchange market is that one cannot expect to earn any speculative profits. Recall that speculation is based upon the trading strategy of buying low and selling high. If there are no exchange rates that are too low, then there is nothing to buy. Neither are there any currencies to sell, since none would have a price that is too high.

Market efficiency does not rule out the possibility of speculative profits. It implies only that one cannot expect to earn speculative profits. If 1,000 individuals try to speculate on currency values, market efficiency implies that 500 will make a profit, some a very large profit, and 500 will incur losses, again some very large. In an efficient market these outcomes are determined by chance and not by ability. On average the profits equal the losses.

Efficiency of the foreign exchange market does not necessarily imply that the future spot rate will on average equal the current spot rate. It implies only that the future spot rate will on average equal the forward rate, the futures price, and the exercise price on "at-the-money" options. We would only expect the future spot rate to equal the current spot rate, if it happens to be equal to the forward rate, the futures price, and the exercise price on at-the-money options.

Unfortunately for potential speculators, most formal statistical studies fail to reject the theory that the foreign exchange market is efficient. Even the studies that do find statistically significant inefficiencies suggest that the magnitude of the inefficiencies, and hence expected speculative profits, are very small.

Ironically, many financial economists attribute the efficiency of the foreign exchange market to the effects of speculative activity. Because speculators buy currencies when their values are too low, they create extra demand that drives the value of the currency up until it is no longer too low. Similarly, when currency values are too high, speculators sell currencies, which creates extra supply and drives their value down until it is no longer too high. Only the speculators who are best informed, quickest to act, and able to trade at the lowest costs can profit before the currencies adjust to their correct prices. It is not surprising that inefficiencies are difficult to find, very temporary, and small in magnitude.

FORECASTS IMPLIED BY THE PARITY CONDITIONS

It is useful to consider a speculator's forecast of the future spot rate to be the speculator's expected future spot rate, since several of the international parity conditions relate the expected future spot rate to the current spot rate and other economic variables. The Unbiased Forward Rate Theory implies that the expected future spot rate equals the forward rate. This is consistent with an efficient foreign exchange market, since one cannot expect an arbitrage profit when the expected buying and selling prices are the same.

Other parity conditions do not necessarily imply the equality of the forward rate and the expected future spot rate. In the following two sections we explore the usefulness of the International Fisher Effect and purchasing power parity for forecasting the future spot rate.

International Fisher Effects

In Chapter 8, we showed that the International Fisher Effect related the ratio of the expected future spot rate and the current spot rate to interest rates in two countries a and b:

$$E\{(A/B)_{t+1}\}/(A/B)_t = (1+ r_a)/(1 + r_b) \qquad [1]$$

Multiplying both sides of this equation by the current spot rate gives us the following estimator of the expected future spot rate:

$$E\{(A/B)_{t+1}\} = (A/B)_t 1+ r_a)/(1 + r_b) \qquad [2]$$

For example, if we wish to forecast the future value of the French franc in dollars, we multiply the current value of the franc ($0.17) by one plus the U.S. interest rate (seven percent) and divide by one plus the French interest rate (nine percent):

$$(\$/FF)_t(1+ r_{us}) \ / \ (1 + r_{fra}) \ = E\{ (\$/FF)_{t+1} \}$$
$$(0.17)(1 + .07) \ / \ (1 + .09) \ = (.1669)$$

and forecast a future price of $0.1669 for the franc.

This is only one of many possible forecasts for the value of the franc that can be obtained from the International Fisher Effect. Equation [2] will remain the same, but forecasters can select from an almost endless variety of interest rates.

If interbank Eurodeposit rates (see Chapter 19) are used for the two interest rates, the forecast is likely to be very close to the forward rate because of the likelihood that interest rate parity holds. The use of other interest rates will result in forecasted future spot rates that can differ significantly from the forward rate. The performance of the forecasting model will depend upon the choice of interest rates used.

Purchasing Power Parity

Purchasing power parity can also be used to develop forecasts of the future spot rate. It equates the ratio of the expected future spot rate and the current spot rate to a function of expected future inflation rates:

$$E\{(A/B)_{t+1}\}/(A/B)_t = (1+E\{p_a\})/(1+E\{p_b\}) \qquad [3]$$

Dividing both sides of this equation by the current spot rate yields the following estimator for the expected future spot rate:

$$E\{(A/B)_{t+1}\} = (A/B)_t (1 + E\{p_a\})/(1 + E\{p_b\}) \qquad [4]$$

For example, if the current value of the French franc is $0.17 and you expect inflation rates of four percent and seven percent in the U.S. and France, respectively, you would forecast a future value of $0.1652 for the franc:

$$(\$/FF)_t(1+E\{p_{us}\})/(1+E\{p_{fra}\}) = E\{(\$/FF)_{t+1}\}$$
$$(0.17)(1+.04)/(1 + .07) = (0.1652)$$

As is the case with forecasting models based on the International Fisher Effect, models based on equation [4] can provide many different forecasts, depending on how the forecaster estimates the expected inflation rates in the two countries.

The simplest type of inflation rate forecast assumes that the expected future inflation rate equals the most recent inflation rate observed. Even in this case there are many inflation rates to choose from such as the *Consumer Price Index*, the *GNP Deflator*, and the *Wholesale Price Index*, along with a host of other special price indexes for particular types of goods and consumers. Many more complex methods for estimating expected inflation rates are outlined in a wide variety of economics texts related to forecasting inflation.

Speculators would be wise to study the advanced statistical techniques for estimating future inflation. The profitability of speculation depends on the quality of the forecasted future spot rate, and the quality of that forecast depends in turn on the quality of the inflation forecasts.

ALTERNATIVE FORECASTING MODELS

One should not get the impression that forecasts of future spot rates must be based on parity conditions or even economic theories. There are an endless variety of forecasting models. One particular class of forecasting models is based upon technical analysis.

Technical analysis refers to the study of past changes in exchange rates in order to forecast future rates. It can range in sophistication from simple charting, which graphs past rates over time in the hope of discovering trends or repetitive patterns in exchange rate movements, to sophisticated time series models such as the autoregressive integrated moving average or Fourier analysis, which fits mathematical equations to even the most complex time series.

Filter rules are another variety of forecasting model that is also frequently used to forecast stock prices. A filter rule can be based upon any type of data and be as complex or simple as desired. Some filter rules rely on an extensive theoretical analysis of relevant variables, while others are based upon little more than casual ad hoc reasoning.

For example, suppose a speculator believes that the values of currencies are positively related to the strength of their respective country's economy. The speculator would obtain as much data as possible on variables that might relate to a country's future economic growth, such as the percentage change in Gross National Product, the national savings rate, and the percent of national income devoted to research and development.

One could begin by ranking countries according to their growth in national income. The lower half of the sample of countries would be discarded (filtered out). The remaining countries could then be ranked according to national savings rates and filtered again. This process could continue until all of the forecaster's economic data are exhausted or all but one of the countries are discarded. The currencies of the countries remaining would be projected to increase in value at the fastest rates.

The variety of filter rules is endless and can incorporate as much or as little formal economic theory as desired. The value of the filter rule can be tested by comparing past forecasts based on the filters to subsequent exchange rate changes.

Exchange rate forecasting models are not limited to the parity conditions, technical analysis, or filter rules described in this chapter to illustrate some of the many approaches to forecasting. Further, the complexity of a forecasting model is not necessarily an indication of its quality. Profitability is the best measure of speculative forecasting.

EVALUATING EXCHANGE RATE FORECASTS

There is no economic theory that can be used to evaluate a forecasting model. Yet speculation based on a bad forecasting model can lead to financial ruin for an investor or a business. Fortunately, forecasting models can be evaluated using past time series of exchange rates without putting the investor's wealth at risk, provided some simple rules are followed in order to avoid drawing the wrong conclusions about a forecasting model.

The first step is to obtain a time series of the exchange rates that you are trying to forecast. If you are forecasting currency values one month into the future, the times series should consist of monthly observations. The time series should end as recently as possible, so that current economic influences on the exchange rate are reflected in the data and you avoid adopting an obsolete forecasting method. The time series should also extend back over a long enough period of time to capture any factors related to the entire business cycle.

Once you have collected the exchange rates, you must also collect either forward rates, futures prices, or option prices for the same periods, depending upon which market you wish to speculate in. Appropriate data can be obtained from public institutions such as the International Monetary Fund and private sources such as the Chicago Mercantile Exchange, DRI, Inc., CompuServe, and many banks and brokerages.

Once you have collected these time series, you must use your forecasting model to generate a matching time series of forecasts for the exchange rate. For each period in the time series, you must obtain a forecast of the exchange rate in the subsequent period.

You must be careful not to use information or data to make a forecast in period "t" that would have become available only in a later period. For example, if you are using purchasing power parity to forecast the value of the Mexican peso on January 1, 1980, be sure to avoid using the actual rates of inflation for 1979, since these would not have been known prior to the start of 1980.

You should also be careful not to inadvertently use your knowledge of economic history when choosing the type of forecasting model. For example, we know that, during the 1980s, Mexico's foreign debt increased and the value of the peso declined. The 1980s would be an unsuitable period over which to test a peso forecasting model based on the level of Mexico's foreign debt.

After the time series are collected and prepared, you simply calculate the profit or loss that you would have obtained by using your forecasts to buy low and sell high. Remember that you cannot buy or sell at the forecasted rate, but only at the subsequent spot rate.

For example, if you generate a forecast on January 1, 1979, of $0.005 for the value of the peso on January 1, 1980, and you contract to buy pesos at the forward rate of $0.004, observed on January 1, 1980, then you must sell them at whatever the spot rate is for January 1, 1980. Keep a running sum of the periodic profits and losses. The quality of the forecast is reflected in total profit earned or loss suffered over the entire time series. Variations in the profits and losses are a measure of the risk of the forecasting model.

CHAPTER PERSPECTIVE
Accurate forecasts of future spot rates can guarantee enormous profits for currency speculators. Exchange rate forecasts, however, are rarely accurate. Speculation can still be profitable, if one can forecast whether future spot rates will be higher or lower than the forward rate, futures price, or exercise price on at-the-money options.

Speculative profits are governed by the extent to which the foreign exchange market is efficient. Only a few statistical studies suggest that speculators can expect to make significant profits. Few financial economists would argue that the foreign exchange market is inefficient.

Forecasters can use the International Fisher Effect and purchasing power parity to forecast exchange rates. In addition, they may use a variety of technical analysis and filter rule techniques. Although forecasting models cannot be evaluated theoretically, there are techniques for testing them with historical data.

Managing Foreign Transaction Exposure

INTRODUCTION AND MAIN POINTS

In Chapter 10 on forecasting exchange rates, we saw that although a wide variety of methods are available, none of them enable us to predict future exchange rates with a great deal of accuracy. Hence, businesses cannot avoid unexpected changes in exchange rates. This chapter is the first of three that address the techniques available to corporate financial managers for managing the risks that arise as a result of exchange rate fluctuations.

There are three types of corporate exposure to exchange rate risk: transaction exposure, translation exposure, and economic exposure. This chapter addresses the nature of transaction exposure and explains the methods for reducing or eliminating it. The next two chapters address translation and economic exposure.

After studying the material in this chapter:

▬ You will understand the nature and consequences of transaction exposure.

▬ You will be able to measure the magnitude of transaction exposure.

▬ You will be able to design strategies for eliminating some transaction exposure.

▬ You will be able to evaluate and select the most appropriate hedging techniques.

▬ You will recognize types of transaction exposures that cannot be eliminated and be able to design strategies for reducing them.

NATURE OF TRANSACTION EXPOSURE

For an American business, *transaction exposure* refers to variability in the dollar value of a known future foreign currency cash flow that results from variability in the future value of the dollar. In the case of a business in another country, it would refer to variability in the value of cash flows in terms of that country's currency.

For example, suppose an American company has sold a shipload of scrap iron to Japan for $150 million yen, but the

Japanese company does not have to pay until the scrap iron arrives in about 30 days. The American company cannot convert the yen into dollars for 30 days and does not know what the value of the yen will be until then. It can forecast the rate, but the forecast is almost certainly not going to be accurate. The range of possible dollar values for the 150 million yen is the measure of the company's transaction exposure.

Transferring Exposure

The simplest method of avoiding transaction exposure is to transfer it to another company. The American scrap iron exporter could quote the sales price of scrap iron for sale in Japan in dollars. Then the Japanese importer would face the transaction exposure resulting from uncertainty about the exchange rate. Another simple means of transferring the risk is to price the scrap iron in yen but demand immediate payment, in which case the current spot rate will determine the dollar value of the export.

The problem with transferring exposure is that the company avoids its difficulties only by imposing them on its customers or its suppliers. In the case of a small or inexperienced company, transferring risk to a large and sophisticated business may be appropriate. In other cases, the practice is likely to result in lost sales or hidden costs.

Net Transaction Exposure

Larger companies that do a continuing and sizable amount of foreign currency transactions may find that much of their exposure to unexpected exchange rate changes nets out over many different transactions. A receivable of 150 million yen owed to an American company in 30 days is much less risky if the American company must pay a different Japanese supplier 100 million yen in 25 days. The risk is reduced even if the business has only receipts in yen on a continuing basis; some of the time the value of the yen will increase unexpectedly, resulting in an unexpected gain, while at other times the yen will decrease, resulting in an unexpected loss.

Transaction exposure is further reduced when payments and receipts are in many different currencies. The values of different foreign currencies are never perfectly correlated. An unexpected increase in the value of the pound may improve the profit margin on receipts from Britain, while an unexpected decrease in the value of the franc may reduce profits on a receipt from France. Although there will always be some remaining net transaction exposure, it may be small enough that the company is best off avoiding the costs of eliminating it completely.

MANAGING SHORT-TERM TRANSACTION EXPOSURE
In the event a company chooses to eliminate transaction exposure, there are a variety of hedging techniques available, if the transaction will take place in less than one year. Companies would do well to price or evaluate the costs of several techniques in order to make an optimal choice.

Forward Contracts
The most direct method of eliminating transaction exposure is to hedge the risk with a forward exchange contract. For example, suppose an American business has sold 1,000 barrels of sulfuric acid to a Mexican company under a sales contract that specifies the payment of 30 million pesos in 30 days. The American producer can eliminate its transaction exposure by selling 30 million pesos to its bank at a 30-day forward rate of 3,000 pesos per dollar. No matter what happens to the exchange rate over the next month, the company is assured of being able to convert the 30 million pesos into $10,000. Conversely, if the company had an account payable instead of a receivable, it could eliminate the transaction exposure by buying the pesos at the forward rate.

In this example, the transaction exposure is eliminated only if the Mexican buyer does not default on its 30-million peso obligation. A default by the Mexican buyer would not relieve the American seller of its obligation to deliver 30 million pesos to the bank in return for $10,000. The American company would have to buy those 30 million pesos at the spot rate one month later.

According to Unbiased Forward Rate Theory, the expected spot rate will be 3,000 pesos per dollar, which means that the probability of a higher rate is no greater than the probability of a lower rate. Unfortunately, what is true on average is rarely true for a specific instance. Hence, the 30 million pesos will almost certainly cost the American company either more or less than $10,000.

Futures Contracts
Many small businesses are not eligible for forward rate contracts except at highly unfavorable terms. Evidence that the bank is quoting unfavorable terms would be a very large spread in the forward rate quote (see Chapter 3). The reason for these unfavorable quotes is that the bank bears the risk that the business will

not fulfill the forward rate contracts. Banks will refuse to offer forward contracts at any rate to uncreditworthy companies. Firms have the option, however, of hedging transaction exposure with futures contracts.

Almost any company and most individuals can trade foreign exchange futures contracts. All that is needed is the initial margin of from $1,000 to $2,000 per contract plus a brokerage account with a net balance of $5,000 to $10,000.

As emphasized in Chapter 3, the potential liability for a futures contract is unlimited. However, if the futures contract is used to hedge transaction exposure, any loss on the futures contract will approximately be offset by a gain on the currency transaction.

In principle, a futures market hedge is no different from a forward market hedge. To illustrate, consider an American business that has an account payable for 62,500 British pounds, due on the third Wednesday of September. The company could buy one September pound futures contract. If the value of the pound increased, the dollar value of the company's account payable would increase, resulting in a reduction in the company's value. However, the value of the futures contract would increase by an equal amount, leaving the net value of the company unchanged. If the value of the pound decreased, the dollar value of the payable account would increase, but the value of the futures contract would decrease by an equal amount.

An American business that has an account receivable for British pounds would hedge its position by selling short the pound futures contract. A short sale of a future contract puts the business in a position opposed to that of a business owning the futures contract. When the futures contract increases in value, the company loses that amount. When the futures contract decreases in value, it gains that amount.

A decrease in the value of the pound would reduce both the dollar value of the receivable and the value of the futures contract. Although the lower value of the receivable reduces the value of the business, the reduction in the value of the futures contract would increase the value of the business, since the short position could be eliminated by buying a pound futures contract at the new lower price. If the value of the pound increases, the business gains on its receivable, but loses an equal amount on its short position in the futures contract because it must buy an offsetting futures contract at the new higher price.

One important disadvantage of using a futures contract is that they are marked to market on a daily basis. Any losses must be made up in cash on a daily basis, while the offsetting gain on the currency transaction will be deferred until the transaction actually occurs. This can create a liquidity crisis for small companies and for individuals.

Another disadvantage of using futures contracts for hedging is that they trade only in standardized amounts and mature on standardized dates. The preceding examples specified that the company would either receive or pay 62,500 pounds on the third Wednesday of September. The resulting hedge was simple, because a futures contract for 62,500 pounds that matures on the third Wednesday of September exists. This happy coincidence rarely occurs outside of textbooks.

When receivables and payables mature at times, and in amounts, that do not coincide with standardized futures contracts, the hedges are not perfect. Changes in the net value of the business that result from exchange rate changes are only partially eliminated, because the change in the value of the futures contract does not precisely match the change in the value of the receivable or payable.

Money Market Hedges

In situations where forward market hedges are not available or too expensive and where a futures market hedge is not feasible or entails too much risk of insolvency, a company should consider a money market hedge. A money market hedge enables a company with a future receivable or a future payable to make the required exchange of currencies at the current spot rate. It is called a *money market hedge* because it requires borrowing or lending in the short-term money market.

For example, suppose an American business expects to receive four million Brazilian cruzeiros in one month from a Brazilian customer. There is no futures contract for the cruzeiro. Furthermore, banks, fearful of foreign exchange controls, quote very large bid/ask spreads on forward rates for the cruzeiro. The business could still eliminate uncertainty about the rate of currency exchange by borrowing 3,636,363 cruzeiros in Brazil at an interest rate of 10 percent per month (inflation and interest rates are extremely high in Brazil):

$$(\text{cruzeiros})_{t+1} \, / \, (1 + r_{bra}) = (\text{cruzeiros})_t$$
$$(4,000,000) \, / \, (1 + .10) = 3,636,363$$

The company can convert the cruzeiros into \$9090.91 at the spot rate of \$0.0025 per cruzeiro as follows:

$$(cruzeiros)_t (dollars/cruzeiro)_t = (dollars)_t$$
$$(3,636,363) (0.0025) = 9090.91$$

When the four million cruzeiro receivable is paid by the Brazilian customer one month later, it is used to pay off the principle and interest accrued on the loan in Brazil:

$$(cruzeiros)_t (1 + r_{bra}) = (cruzeiros)_{t+1}$$
$$(3,636,363) (1 + .10) = 4,000,000$$

If the American company had an account payable in cruzeiros in Brazil, it could also use a money market hedge by borrowing dollars in the U.S., converting them into cruzeiros at the spot rate, and then investing the cruzeiros in Brazil until the payable is due.

The cost of a money market hedge is the difference between the borrowing and the lending interest rates. Most companies and individuals must pay more to borrow funds than they can receive when they lend funds. Banks must lend funds at a higher interest rate than they pay for funds in order to earn a profit. They demand an even higher interest rate if there is any risk of default. In order to reduce the risk, banks often require borrowers to pledge the receivable as collateral on the loan. If the receivable presents a low risk, the bank will require a lower interest rate. If the business is borrowing for a future payable, it can pledge the cruzeiro deposit as collateral.

When the risk to the bank is low, the company's borrowing and lending rates are close to the risk-free rate. In this case, a money market hedge may be the least costly hedging technique even if forward rates and futures contracts are available. As explained in Chapter 7, the forward rate is often determined by interest rate parity, which is based upon risk-free borrowing and lending.

Use of Options

Hedging transaction exposure in either the forward market, the futures market, or the money market reduces uncertainty about the business' future value by fixing the rate at which currencies will be exchanged. When subsequent changes in currency values are unfavorable, the hedge prevents a reduction in the value of the business. However, the hedge also prevents an increase in the value of the business, when the currency change is favorable. Hedging in the options market enables businesses and individuals to reduce losses caused by unfavorable exchange rate changes, while preserving gains from favorable exchange rate changes.

Like futures contracts, currency option contracts specify the future exchange of currencies at a specified rate and are standardized with respect to maturity and amount. In fact, the most widely traded options are on the futures contract rather than the currency itself.

Unlike futures contracts, however, options contracts are rights, not obligations. If the exchange rate moves in a direction that is disadvantageous to the owner of an option, he or she does not have to carry out the exchange.

When used to hedge transaction exposure, the option can be enforced to protect the value of the business from losses without reducing or sacrificing possible gains. If the change in the dollar value of the receivable or payable is unfavorable, the option can be enforced. If the change in the value of the receivable or payable is favorable, the option can be discarded. Options enable businesses and investors to restrict potential losses without restricting potential gains. But, as we will show, this flexibility has a cost.

As an illustration, consider an American importer that must pay a Japanese company 6,250,000 yen on the third Wednesday of December. Management wants to protect the buyer from large losses that would be incurred if the value of the yen increases before the obligation is paid.

The current value of the yen is $0.0072, so the importer buys a December call option for 6,250,000 yen at an exercise price of $0.0072 per yen. In addition to the broker's commission of $25.00 the importer must pay a premium of $0.00015 per yen or $937.50 { = (0.0015) (6,250,000) }.

If by the third Wednesday in December the value of the yen falls to $0.0068, then the American business discards the option and buys the 6,250,000 yen at the new spot rate for $42,500:

$$(\text{yen}) \, (\text{dollars/yen}) = (\text{dollars})$$
$$(6{,}250{,}000) \, (0.0068) = 42{,}500$$

The total cost to the company would be $43,462.50:

$$(\text{commission}) + (\text{premium}) + (\text{cost of exercise}) = (\text{total})$$
$$(25.00) \quad + \; (937.50) \; + \quad (42{,}500) \quad = 43{,}462.50$$

If the value of the yen rises above $0.0072, the company exercises the call option and buys the 6,250,000 yen at the exercise price of $0.0072 per yen and pays $45,000 to satisfy the account payable:

$$\text{(yen) (dollars/yen)} = \text{(dollars)}$$
$$(6,250,000)(0.0072) = 45,000$$

The total cost to the company never exceeds $45,962.50

$$\text{(commission)} + \text{(premium)} + \text{(cost of exercise)} = \text{(total)}$$
$$(25.00) \quad + \quad (937.50) + \quad (45,000) \quad = 45,962.50$$

but the cost may be much less depending on how low the value of the yen falls.

In the event the importer has a receivable account denominated in yen, it can purchase a yen put option. The put option gives the importer the right to sell the yen that it receives to the writer of the option at the exercise price specified in the option contract. Hence, the company is guaranteed a minimum total dollar amount in the future that is equal to the exercise value of the option less the premium and commission paid for the put option. If the value of the yen rises, the firm discards the put option and receives the new dollar value of the yen receivable less the amount of premium and commission paid on the option.

While option hedges appear to place the company in a no-lose situation, the actual benefits of option hedges are more in doubt. Regardless of whether the option is exercised, the company always bears the full cost of the option premium and commission. In effect, the company substitutes an unknown and potentially disastrous loss with a smaller, but certain, cost.

In this sense, an option hedge is very similar to the purchase of insurance. (In fact, option models can be used to estimate insurance premiums.) The total benefit of an option hedge involves a trade-off between avoiding risk of potential losses and the certain monetary cost of the option. If the option market is efficient, the net monetary benefit of an option hedge to the company is neglible or even slightly negative due to transaction costs. The gain to the company is the reduction in uncertainty.

One can understand the efficiency of the option market better if one considers options from the point of view of the seller or writer of the option. The writer of an option has no upside potential but unlimited downside potential. The only way a buyer can induce someone to write an option is to pay a sufficient premium. Hence option premiums reflect an equilibrium at which the buyer and the seller of the option both feel their interests are protected.

If we argue that options provide a substantial net benefit to their owners, then we must conclude that the sellers of the options are voluntarily agreeing to substantial net losses. If we argue that the sellers obtain a benefit, then we must conclude the buyers are agreeing to suffer losses. Advocates of an efficient option market conclude that neither party wins or loses consistently and that the premium is the correct compensation for any differences in expected payoffs.

Cross Hedging

In all of the methods of hedging transaction exposure that have been discussed so far, it has been assumed that a market exists for either forward rates, futures contracts, credit, or options in the foreign currency that is being hedged. This is not always true, especially in the case of small developing countries. In such cases, cross hedging offers companies and investors a means of reducing transaction exposure.

Cross hedging refers to a hedge that is constructed in a currency whose value is highly correlated with the value of the currency in which the receivable or payable is denominated. In some cases, it is relatively easy to find highly correlated currencies, because many smaller countries try to peg (fix) the exchange rate between their currency and some major currency such as the dollar, the pound, or the European Currency Unit. One should remember, however, that these currencies are not perfectly correlated, because efforts to peg values frequently fail.

To illustrate, suppose that a company has a payable or a receivable denominated in the currency of a small African nation for which there are no developed currency or credit markets. The company would explore the possibility that the currency is pegged to the value of a major currency. If not, the company would look at past changes in the value of the currency to see if they are correlated with changes in the value of any major currency. The company would then engage in either a forward market, futures market, money market, or options market hedge in the major currency that is most closely related to the small African currency.

The success or failure of cross hedging depends upon the extent to which the major currency changes in value along with the minor currency. Although cross hedging is an imperfect means of reducing transaction exposure, sometimes it is the only method available.

MANAGING LONG-TERM TRANSACTION EXPOSURE

In theory, the same techniques used to hedge short-term transaction exposure can be used to hedge long-term transaction exposure. Several large multinational banks have offered long-term forward exchange contracts with maturities as long as seven years, but only the largest and most creditworthy corporate customers qualify for such contracts.

At present there are no markets for currency futures options with maturities greater than one year. Although individual companies can negotiate a currency option contract, there is no secondary market for the instrument. Hence, a number of alternative hedging techniques have developed for reducing long-term transaction exposure. These are explained in the following sections.

Parallel Loans

Multinational corporations can often reduce each other's long-term transaction exposure by entering into an arrangement known as a *parallel* or *back-to-back loan*. For example, suppose an American company wants to invest in a project in France that will repay the investment and earnings in francs over the next ten years. The American investor is confident of the rate of return in francs, but wants to avoid the risk that the value of the franc in dollars will decline unexpectedly, resulting in a negative return in dollars. If it can find a French company that wants to make a similarly sized investment in the U.S., it can arrange offsetting loans. That is, the French company will lend the American company francs and the American company will lend the French company dollars with which to make their respective investments. The American company will repay the French firm with its franc earnings, and the French company will repay the American firm with its dollar earnings.

In this arrangement, neither company will have to exchange currencies in the foreign exchange market. Hence, they are both unaffected by exchange rate changes. However, both are exposed to default risk, since the failure of one company to repay its loan does not relieve the other of its obligation.

Currency Swaps

The credit risk associated with a parallel loan can be avoided by the use of a currency swap. A *currency swap* is an agreement by two companies to exchange specified amounts of currency now and to reverse the exchange at some point in the future.

The rates at which the currencies are exchanged can differ if both parties expect the values of currencies to change over time. The practical effect of a currency swap is almost identical to a parallel loan except that the parties do not have to record the loans as financial assets and liabilities on their balance sheets and neither incurs much credit risk.

The absence of much credit risk grows out of the nature of a currency swap. Default on a currency swap means that the currencies are not exchanged in the future, while default on a parallel loan means that the loan is not repaid. Default on a currency swap entails no loss of investment or earnings; the only consequence is that the companies must exchange the foreign currency in the foreign exchange market at the new exchange rate. On the other hand, if one loan is not repaid, the other party loses its investment and earnings.

Credit Swaps

Multinational banks act as brokers in trying to find and match partners in parallel loans and currency swaps. It is often very difficult to find companies whose needs perfectly offset one another, so these techniques are often imperfect and only partially reduce the transaction exposure. In cases where partners cannot be matched, a credit swap is often useful. *Credit swaps* involve a deposit in one currency and a loan in another. The deposit is returned after the loan is repaid.

For example, an American business could deposit dollars in the New York branch of a Mexican bank, which would in turn lend the depositor pesos for an investment in Mexico. After the Mexican loan is repaid in pesos, the dollar deposit would be returned. Although a credit swap eliminates transaction exposure on funds invested, the earnings are largely exposed.

CHAPTER PERSPECTIVE

Transaction exposure refers to the risk that a business or individual incurs when future payments or receipts are denominated in foreign currencies whose future values are uncertain. This risk can be eliminated by using contracts to lock in the ratio at which these future foreign currency receipts or payments are to be exchanged. A wide variety of contractual arrangements have evolved because there are always circumstances that can prevent parties to these contracts from fulfilling their obligations.

Short-term transaction exposure is the easiest to avoid or reduce. Hedging arrangements include transactions in the forward market, money market, futures market, and options market. In situations where markets do not exist, cross hedges can be obtained by using contracts in currencies whose values tend to be related.

Long-term hedges are more expensive and difficult to arrange. Techniques such as parallel loans, currency swaps, and credit swaps reduce, but do not eliminate transaction exposure. Frequently, the companies and individuals are forced to choose between incurring some transaction exposure or credit risk.

Managing Translation Exposure

INTRODUCTION AND MAIN POINTS

This chapter addresses translation exposure, the second type of risk to which businesses are subjected by unexpected changes in exchange rates. Translation refers to the conversion of a company's financial statements from one currency into another, and translation exposure is the variability in the company's reported financial condition that results from changes in the exchange rate that is used to translate statements.

There is no "correct" way of translating financial statements. Different countries specify different accounting techniques. In the U.S., the choice of techniques changed in the 1970s and again in the 1980s. Hence, we briefly review some of the different techniques for translating financial statements. Afterwards, we focus in more detail on the method presently used in the U.S.

After studying the material in this chapter:

■ You will understand the nature and causes of translation exposure.

■ You will understand the rationale behind different methods for translating financial statements.

■ You will recognize flaws in the monetary/nonmonetary method.

■ You will recognize flaws in the current/noncurrent method.

■ You will be familiar with the basic accounting rules specified by FASB 52 as it is currently required for U.S. businesses.

NATURE OF TRANSLATION EXPOSURE

Companies must report their financial statements in units of their own country's currency. American businesses report in dollars, Japanese businesses report in yen, and so on. This presents a problem for multinational businesses that have assets and/or liabilities in different countries.

Foreign assets and liabilities typically are valued in the currencies of the countries in which they are located. Multinational corporations must convert these foreign currency values into a common currency in order to prepare their financial statements. *Translation* is the term used for the process of converting reported values on financial statements from one currency into another.

We use exchange rates to translate financial statements. Unexpected changes in exchange rates create unexpected changes in the reported financial condition of the company. Translation exposure refers to variability in accounting values for a company's profit and net worth that results from variations in exchange rates.

The nature of translation exposure is complicated by national differences in accounting standards used to translate financial statements. Many, if not most, values reported on a company's financial statement are based upon historic rather than current value. Hence, it can be logically argued that historic rather than current exchange rates should be used to translate them. Unfortunately, there is little agreement on how to apply this principle to specific items on the income statement and balance sheet. As a result, different countries have adopted different accounting standards and modified them over time.

ALTERNATIVE METHODS OF TRANSLATION

Because the nature of translation exposure depends upon the method of translation, it is necessary to be familiar with the basic alternative methods of translation. The following section describes the three most common methods, all of which are currently used in some countries. Each of the three has constituted the basic method of translation in the U.S. at one time or another.

Current/Noncurrent Method

The *current/noncurrent method*, sometimes called the *net working capital method*, translates current assets and liabilities at the current exchange rate and translates long-term assets and liabilities at the historic exchange rate. The historic exchange rate is the value of the currency at the time the assets or liabilities are originally recorded. The rationale behind this practice is that, since long-term assets and liabilities are recorded at historic or book value rather than at their current value, it would be inappropriate to use the current exchange rate.

Income statement items are translated at the average exchange rate for the period over which the income statement is computed. An exception to this rule requires that income statement items reflecting changes in the balance sheet (such as cost of goods sold, which reflects inventory changes) be translated at the same rate used for the balance sheet item. Likewise, interest on bonds is translated at the historic exchange rate for the bonds.

Wide fluctuations in exchange rates can result in wide fluctuations in reported profits, even if profits prior to translation did not change. Net worth must equal the difference between assets and liabilities at all times. For example, consider the balance sheet of the German subsidiary of an American company that has no change in its balance sheet items as recorded in deutsche marks but shows the translation effects of an increase in the value of the deutsche mark from $0.50 in 1990 to $0.55 in 1991.

TABLE 12–1
Income Statement

	Deutsche Mark		U.S. Dollars	
	1990	1991	1990	1991
Current Assets	200	200	100	110
Fixed Assets	200	200	100	100
Total Assets	400	400	200	210
Current Liabilities	100	100	50	55
L. T. Liabilities	200	200	100	100
Total Liabilities	300	300	150	155
Net Worth	100	100	50	55

The dollar value of the net worth increases by 10 percent as a result of the 10 percent increase in the value of the deutsche mark. This increase in net worth is reported on the income statement as profit. However, if a company has positive net working capital (current assets less current liabilities), it may finance with long-term debt. For example, consider the same company with no current liabilities.

TABLE 12–2
Balance Sheet

	Deutsche Mark		U.S. Dollars	
	1990	1991	1990	1991
Current Assets	200	200	100	110
Fixed Assets	200	200	100	100
Total Assets	400	400	200	210
Current Liabilities	0	0	0	0
L. T. Liabilities	300	300	150	150
Total Liabilities	300	300	150	150
Net Worth	100	100	50	60

The net worth has now increased by 20 percent as a result of the same 10 percent increase in the value of the deutsche mark. This phenomenon results from translating the net working capital at the higher current exchange rate, while translating the offsetting long-term liability at the historic rate. The resultant artificial change in net worth distorts the reported profits of the business. While this distortion overstates profits when the foreign currency appreciates, it understates profits when the foreign currency depreciates.

Monetary/Nonmonetary Method

Since most American companies maintain positive net working capital, the current/noncurrent method of translation caused a lot of dissatisfaction after exchange rates were allowed to float in the early 1970s. In December 1974, the Financial Accounting Standards Board (FASB) adopted FASB 8, which required American businesses to translate according to the *monetary/non-monetary method*.

Under FASB 8, monetary assets such as cash, marketable securities, and accounts receivable are translated at current exchange rates. Nonmonetary assets, which include fixed assets and inventory, are translated at historic exchange rates. Monetary liabilities, which include current liabilities and long-term debt, are translated at current rates.

Because long-term debt was translated at the current exchange rate, the problem with the current/noncurrent method of translation is avoided. However, translating inventory at historic rates still creates artificial fluctuations in translated net worth and reported profits. The distortion is not great for businesses that rely on FIFO (first-in-first-out) inventory accounting, since inventory is typically short-lived and the difference between the current and historic exchange rate is not great.

Unfortunately, the effects of inflation and taxation have forced many companies to switch to LIFO (last-in-first-out) inventory accounting, and exchange rates have became more volatile. Hence, older inventory is carried on the balance sheet, and the discrepancy between historic and current exchange rates increases. Dissatisfaction with FASB 8 led to the adoption of FASB 52 in December 1981.

Current Rate Method

The distortions that result from the current/noncurrent and monetary/nonmonetary methods can be avoided by simply translating all balance sheet and income statement items at the current rate. This technique is called the *current rate method* or sometimes the *all-accounts method*. This method is used by most British companies and is recommended by the Institutes of Chartered Accountants in England and Scotland.

Unfortunately, the current rate method of translation conflicts with the theory of historic rate accounting, which underlies accounting practice in the U.S. Accounting theorists object to applying current exchange rates to balance sheet items that are recorded at historic cost as opposed to current value.

Temporal Method

The conflict with historic rate accounting led many accountants to seek an alternative to the current rate method. Since most of the objections to the monetary/nonmonetary method revolved around inventory, a compromise was sought.

Most accounting theorists prefer the temporal method of translation. Under the *temporal method*, a company translates its balance sheet and income statements in the same manner as the monetary/nonmonetary method with the exception of inventory. Inventory is translated at the historic rate if it is recorded at historic cost and at the current rate if it is carried at current value.

APPLICATION OF FASB 52

American businesses are currently governed by the translation rules specified in FASB 52. While it is likely that these rules may be modified in the future to conform more closely to the temporal method, no changes are likely in the near term. FASB 52 constitutes an eclectic approach to translation and does not conform entirely to any theoretical approach. Hence, it is necessary to be familiar with several of its basic features.

Determination of the Functional Currency

Under FASB 52 businesses must determine their reporting and functional currencies. The *reporting currency* is simply the currency of the country in which the parent company lists its stock; thus for American companies it is the dollar. The determination of the functional currencies is more complex.

Each foreign subsidiary of the parent company must have a functional currency specified. This *functional currency* is the currency in which most of the subsidiary's operations are carried out. An exception to this rule is subsidiaries that operate in hyperinflationary countries; these subsidiaries must use the dollar as their functional currency. Hyperinflation is defined as an inflation rate above 100 percent.

For foreign subsidiaries that import, export, and/or finance their operations outside of the country in which they are physically located, companies have some discretion with regard to which currency is specified as the functional currency, but they must justify the choice in accordance with FASB 52 guidelines relating to factors such as the responsiveness of the subsidiary's prices to exchange rate changes and the degree of intracorporate transactions, in addition to measures of the degree of foreign as opposed to domestic activities.

For example, most German subsidiaries of American companies would use the deutsche mark as the functional currency. However, German subsidiaries that depended primarily upon supplies produced by the parent company in the U.S. and varied their product prices in Germany according to fluctuations in the dollar value of the deutsche mark could justify using the dollar as their functional currency under FASB 52 guidelines.

Translating When the Foreign Currency Is the Functional Currency

Suppose the German subsidiary of an American company uses the deutsche mark as its functional currency. The income statement and balance sheet will first be prepared in deutsche marks. Items on the income statement are then translated into the reporting currency at the average value of the exchange rate over the period for which the income statement is prepared. The following table provides an example, assuming an average value for the deutsche mark of $0.50.

TABLE 12–3
Income Statement

	Deutsche Marks	U.S. Dollars
Revenues	1000	500
Cost of Goods Sold	500	250
Administrative Expense	100	50
Depreciation	100	50
Earnings Before Interest and Tax	300	150
Interest	100	50
Income Tax	80	40
Net Income	120	60

When the functional currency is the foreign currency, all assets and liabilities are translated at the current exchange rate. The par value, paid-in-surplus, and retained earnings are translated at historic rates. A *cumulative translation adjustment account* is created under net worth so that the basic accounting identity between assets, liabilities, and net worth can be maintained and gains and losses from translating the balance sheet can be kept off the income statement. The following table provides an example, assuming a current value for the deutsche mark of $0.55. The example also assumes that the deutsche mark was worth $0.40 when the stock was sold and $0.45 when previous earnings were retained.

TABLE 12–4
Balance Sheet

	Deutsche Marks	U.S. Dollars
Cash and Marketable Securities	100	55
Accounts Receivable	100	55
Inventory	200	110
Current Assets	400	220
Net Fixed Assets	300	165
Total Assets	700	385
Current Liabilities	200	110
Long-Term Liabilities	200	110
Par Value and Paid-In-Surplus	200	80
Retained Earnings	100	45
Cumulative Translation Adjustment		40
Total Liabilities and Net Worth	700	385

Because assets exceed liabilities, the increase in the value of the deutsche mark increases the net worth in dollars of the German subsidiary. If the value of the deutsche mark declined, the reduction in the dollar value of the net worth would have appeared as a negative value in the cumulative translation adjustment account.

Translating When the Dollar Is the Functional Currency

Companies that are able to specify the dollar as the functional currency of their subsidiaries can translate their financial statements according to the previous methods specified in FASB 8. For the balance sheet, monetary items are translated at the current exchange rate, while par and surplus values of common stock, fixed assets, and inventory are translated at historic rates. The following table translates the balance sheet for the same German subsidiary, assuming that the dollar is the functional currency. It assumes that the fixed assets are booked at the same time as the stock is issued and, hence, are translated at the same rate, $0.40 per mark.

TABLE 12–5
Balance Sheet

	Deutsche Marks	U.S. Dollars
Cash and Marketable Securities	100	55
Accounts Receivable	100	55
Inventory	200	90
Current Assets	400	200
Net Fixed Assets	300	120
Total Assets	700	320
Current Liabilities	200	110
Long-Term Liabilities	200	110
Par Value and Paid-In-Surplus	200	80
Retained Earnings	100	20
Total Liabilities and Net Worth	700	320

There is no cumulative translation adjustment account. Gains or losses resulting from exchange rate changes result in changes in Retained Earnings that must be reflected on the income statement.

The income statement is also translated in accordance with the rules for FASB 8. Revenues, administrative expenses, taxes, and interest are translated at the average exchange rate for the period. *Cost-of-goods-sold* and *depreciation* are translated at the historic rates for inventory and fixed assets, respectively. The following table translates the income statement for the same German subsidiary when the dollar is specified as the functional currency.

TABLE 12–6
Income Statement

	Deutsche Marks	U.S. Dollars
Revenues	1000	500
Cost of Goods Sold	500	225
Administrative Expense	100	50
Depreciation	100	40
Earnings Before Interest and Tax	300	185
Interest	100	50
Income Tax	80	40
Net Income	120	95

Although the use of the dollar as the functional currency increases the dollar value of the net income, it reduces the dollar value of the net worth. If the deutsche mark's dollar value had declined, these outcomes would be reversed.

HEDGING TRANSLATION EXPOSURE

Techniques for hedging translation exposure fall into two categories. The first involves matching assets and liabilities. If the foreign currency is the functional currency for a subsidiary, then all assets and liabilities are translated at current exchange rates. Variability in net worth can be reduced by ensuring that current assets in a particular currency are financed (matched) by current liabilities in that same currency. Variability in net worth is also reduced by financing fixed assets with long-term liabilities in the same currency. If the dollar is the functional currency, then fixed assets are translated at historic rates and long-term liabilities are translated at current rates. Hence, matching currencies actually increases translation exposure.

The second approach to managing translation exposure involves constructing hedges similar to those used to control transaction exposure, such as forward rate contracts, currency futures, and option contracts. In cases where these are not available, companies can rely on some form of cross hedging.

The problem with hedging translation exposure is that the hedge results in a cash gain or loss that is offset by a book value gain or loss that may not always reflect a true economic value. For this reason, many financial economists recommend that companies ignore translation exposure and devote their attention to managing economic exposure, which is the subject of the next chapter.

CHAPTER PERSPECTIVE

Translation exposure refers to the effect of exchange rate changes on a multinational company's consolidated financial statements. The degree and type of exposure depends upon the method used to translate income statements and balance sheets, prepared in one currency into another currency. The major approaches used to translate financial statements include the current/noncurrent method, the monetary/nonmonetary method, and the current rate method. The method chosen differs among countries and changes over time. In the U.S., all three techniques have been utilized at one time or another since the 1960s.

Current accounting practice in the U.S. is governed by FASB 52. Under this rule companies must choose a functional currency for their foreign subsidiaries. If a subsidiary's revenues and expenses are incurred primarily in a foreign currency, then the foreign currency is the functional currency. If the foreign currency experiences hyperinflation, then the functional currency is the dollar. Changes in net worth resulting from translating assets and liabilities at current rates are recorded in a special balance sheet account for translation adjustment and not recorded as a profit or loss on the income statement.

Managing translation exposure consists of matching the currencies of cash inflows and outflows or hedging in the forward, futures, or options markets. Many financial economists recommend that companies avoid hedging translation exposure.

Managing Economic Exposure

INTRODUCTION AND MAIN POINTS

Chapters 11 and 12 addressed the impact of exchange rate changes on a company's accounting statements and foreign currency transactions. This chapter explores the effect of exchange rate changes on the overall value of the business. While transaction exposure and translation exposure are relevant only to businesses engaged in foreign trade or multinational operations, economic exposure is also relevant to companies that are not engaged in foreign commerce.

We begin by defining economic exposure and relating it to translation and transaction exposure. Its nature is then explored with respect to multinational, import-export, and domestic firms. We conclude with a review of strategies and techniques managing economic exposure.

After studying the material in this chapter:

■ You will understand economic exposure as it relates to multinational, import-export, and purely domestic operations.

■ You will be able to evaluate the relevance of transaction and translation exposure as they relate to the value of the business.

■ You will be able to measure the degree of a company's economic exposure to changes in various exchange rates.

■ You will understand the economic factors that cause the value of the business to increase or decrease in response to exchange rate changes.

■ You will be able to devise strategies for controlling the degree of economic exposure to exchange rate changes.

UNDERSTANDING ECONOMIC EXPOSURE

Economic exposure is the broadest measure of exchange rate risk. In a sense it is inclusive of both transaction and translation exposure. The following sections explain the nature and causes of economic exposure, which is then related to transaction and translation exposure.

Nature of Economic Exposure

Economic exposure refers to changes in the value of the company that result from changes in exchange rates. The value of the company is the market price of the stock times the number of shares of stock outstanding. The market price of the stock is the price at which the supply and demand for it is equal. No one thinks the stock is worth more and is not willing to pay more for it. Likewise, no one thinks the stock is worth less and is willing to sell it.

When investors attempt to estimate the worth of a stock, they try to ascertain the company's future earnings. They must consider both the growth and the uncertainty of future earnings. These estimates are then discounted for the effects of time and uncertainty in order to determine the inherent value of the stock. If investors' estimate of inherent value exceeds the market price, they buy the stock. If the estimate of inherent value is below market price, they sell the stock.

In a formal mathematical analysis, the discounted estimate of a stock's value (V) is the present value of all expected future cash flows (C_t) to the investors who own the stock:

$$V = C_1/(1 + k) + C_2/(1 + k)^2 + \ldots + C_n/(1+k)^n$$

where k is the investor's required rate of return and the subscripts on the cash flows indicate the period in which they are received. In an efficient market, a stock's market price equals its value (V). A change in exchange rates influences the market value of a company when it affects the expected future cash flows to the company's investors.

Causes of Economic Exposure

An understanding of the causes of economic exposure requires an analysis of the effect of exchange rates on the expected future cash flows to the company's investors. The impact of a given change in a particular exchange rate depends upon the specific characteristics of the company. This can be understood by examining three types of businesses: a multinational corporation, an importer/exporter, and a purely domestic business.

A multinational corporation typically invests and finances in several countries. Suppose an American electronics conglomerate builds a factory in Italy to produce a patented power transformer for the Italian market. The Italian subsidiary's revenues and expenses are incurred in Italy and denominated in lire. The American owners' expected future cash flows denominated in lire must be converted into dollars at the expected future value of the lira in dollars.

As shown in our discussion of the international parity conditions, the expected future value of the lira depends upon relative interest rates and inflation rates in the U.S. and Italy, along with the current value of the lira. Suppose the current value of the lira increases by 10 percent, but relative interest rates and expected future inflation rates do not change. The expected future dollar value of all expected future cash flows from the Italian subsidiary will increase by 10 percent. Hence, the market value of the Italian subsidiary will increase by 10 percent. If the current value of the lira had decreased by five percent, the value of the subsidiary would have decreased by five percent. Given the assumptions in this example, we see that the value of a foreign subsidiary varies precisely with the current spot rate for the foreign currency.

Companies without foreign subsidiaries also bear economic exposure to exchange rate changes. Consider an American importer of automobiles produced in Korea by a Korean manufacturer. Suppose that the Korean manufacturer sells autos to the American importer at a fixed price in won (W 7,500,000). Suppose that the value of the dollar is 750 won and that the importer is able to pay the Korean manufacturer an equivalent dollar value ($10,000) and then sell the autos to American dealers at a 10 percent markup ($11,000). The importer's owners earn $1,000 per auto.

Now suppose that the current value of the won increases by five percent. The dollar cost of each auto to the importer will rise by five percent to $10,500. If the importer is unable to raise the dollar price of the autos to the dealers, profit on each auto will fall by 50 percent to $500. In the absence of any other changes, the 10 percent increase in the value of the won reduces the dollar value of the expected future cash flows to the importer's owners by 50 percent. Given the same conditions, a small decrease in value of the won would lead to a large increase in the value of the American importer.

Even companies that are not engaged in foreign commerce suffer from economic exposure to exchange rate fluctuations. Consider a small American food processor that specializes in dairy products and that has no interest in foreign operations or in importing and exporting. Assume that it is able to earn a profit margin of 20 percent on sales. Suppose the dollar value of the French franc falls by 20 percent. A French producer of the same dairy products can now sell similar goods in America at a dollar price that is 20 percent lower without reducing its revenues in francs.

Suppose that the American company finds that it must reduce its prices by 10 percent in order to stay competitive with imports from the French supplier. In the absence of other changes, the profit margin of the American company will be cut in half. All expected future cash flows to the company's owners are reduced by 50 percent as a result of the change in the exchange rate. Similarly, an increase in the value of the French franc would induce an increase in the value of the American company.

These three examples are by no means inclusive of all the causes of economic exposure. They serve only to explain how exchange rate changes can affect the market value of any company. Later in this chapter, we will cover other examples of economic exposure.

ECONOMIC VERSUS TRANSACTION AND TRANSLATION EXPOSURE

Transaction exposure can be thought of as a very limited and specific form of economic exposure. Consider the previous example of the American importer of Korean autos. If the American importer had contracted to purchase a fixed number of autos at a specific price in won, the transaction exposure to changes in the value of the won would also be considered economic exposure. But, whereas the transaction exposure would be limited to the contractual obligation to purchase a specific number of cars, the economic exposure would also include the effect of the exchange rate change on any future unplanned imports.

Economic exposure also includes translation exposure to the extent that changes in the business's accounting values affect its market value. In some cases, a change in accounting value of net worth or net income correlates with a change in the company's market value. However, this is often not the case. Accounting values are based upon historic cost, whereas market values are based upon anticipation of future cash flows.

Accounting and market values can diverge. Obsolescence can rapidly reduce an asset's market value, even though its book value remains unchanged. Market conditions can also increase market value of such assets as real estate to well above book value. Translation can increase or reduce these divergences, depending upon economic factors related to exchange rate changes.

Consider a German subsidiary of an American company that is financed with long-term bonds sold in America. The dollar value of the net worth of this subsidiary will increase as the value of the deutsche mark increases, since the assets will be translated at the higher value of the deutsche mark, while the dollar value of the long-term debt will remain unchanged. It is possible, however, that the economic value of the German subsidiary in dollars will remain unchanged. Suppose the value of the deutsche mark rose because the American inflation rate was much higher than the German inflation rate and purchasing power parity held. The increase in the dollar value of the German subsidiary would be an illusion, since historic cost accounting fails to recognize the slower growth in the deutsche mark value of the assets that results from the lower rate of inflation in Germany.

MEASURING ECONOMIC EXPOSURE

Because of differences between economic and accounting values, we need an alternative method of measuring economic exposure. A common approach is to assume that the market value of the company (V) is linearly related to the value of the currency ($/X):

$$V = b_0 + b_1 (\$/X)$$

where b_0 is that portion of the value of the company that is invariant to changes in the value of the currency and b_1 is the change in the value of the company per unit change in the value of the currency. Since it is likely that the value of some companies is linearly related to the values of several currencies ($/X_1$, $/X_2$, $/X_3$, etc.), we generally express the linear relationship as

$$V = b_0 + b_1 (\$/X_1) + b_2 (\$/X_2) + \ldots + b_n (\$/X_n)$$

where b_n is the change in the value of the company per unit change in the value of currency n. The economic exposure of the business to each currency is represented by its respective coefficient (b_1, b_2, etc.).

These coefficients, which constitute measures of the company's economic exposure, can be easily estimated by running a multiple regression analysis on a past time series of the market value of the company, along with the market value of the currencies. For example, suppose you were to collect the following time series of the market values of a company's stock (V), along with the value of the Japanese yen, the British pound, and the German mark:

TABLE 13–1

Date	V	$/Yen	$/Pound	$/Mark
1980	$55	$.005	$1.90	$.45
1981	56	.006	1.70	.40
1982	48	.006	1.80	.42
1983	60	.004	1.60	.48
...	...	...	...	...

You could use simple spreadsheet software such as Lotus 1-2-3 or a financial calculator to regress the stock price on the currency values. You would obtain estimates for the coefficients (bn) that measure economic exposure.

Suppose you obtained the following coefficient estimates from regressing the stock price on the currency values:

TABLE 13–2

b_0	b_{yen}	b_{pound}	b_{mark}
25	4000	0	–500

These results indicate that $25 of the stock's value is invariant to changes in these exchange rates. The yen coefficient implies that an increase of $0.001 in the value of the yen would increase the company's stock by $4.00 $\{= (4000)(.001)\}$.

A similar reduction in the value of the yen would reduce the value of the company's stock by the same amount. The pound coefficient implies that changes in the value of the pound would have no effect on the market value of the company. The negative coefficient on the mark implies that an increase in the value of the mark of $0.01 would reduce the value of the company's stock by $5.00 $\{= (-500)(.01)\}$. A reduction in the value of the mark would increase the value of the company by an amount equal to the coefficient times the change in the mark's value.

Although linear regression is the most common method for estimating a company's economic exposure to exchange rates, it is an imperfect technique. This method assumes that the company's value is linearly related to the currency values. In fact, this is only approximately true. The method also implies that the change in the value of the company is always the same for a given change in the currency value and that the change holds true over extended periods of time. If you have reason to suspect that your company is not linearly related to currency values or that the relationship varies over time, you must use much more sophisticated nonlinear regression and time series analyses.

METHODS OF REDUCING ECONOMIC EXPOSURE
The nature of economic exposure is much more complex than that of either transaction or translation exposure. Many different factors contribute to a company's sensitivity to exchange rates. It is more difficult to measure economic exposure accurately, so analysts must settle for estimates. When you are uncertain about the cause and magnitude of a company's exposure, hedging strategies

are much more problematic. An inappropriate hedge can increase a company's economic exposure. Hence, strategies for hedging economic exposure are neither precise nor always effective.

Matching Cash Flows

In an efficient market, changes in a company's market value reflect changes in the risk-adjusted present value of the company's expected future cash flows to its owners. Hence, for an American business, reducing economic exposure is tantamount to reducing variability in the dollar value of the business's expected future cash flows. Recognition of this leads to strategies for matching the sensitivities of cash inflows and outflows to various currency changes.

For example, suppose an American company has a subsidiary that will generate revenues in Mexican pesos. The sensitivity to the peso exchange rate of the dollar value of the subsidiary's net cash flow to its American owners can be reduced by incurring as many of the subsidiary's expenses in pesos as possible. Where feasible, the subsidiary should purchase supplies and obtain financing in Mexico. In this way, variability in the dollar value of the net cash flow is reduced regardless of the magnitude of the cash flows.

Global Diversification

Another approach to hedging economic exposure is global diversification, which entails expanding the company's markets and production facilities worldwide. If the real exchange rate (see Chapter 8) falls in a particular country, then the company can increase production in that location and boost exports to countries where the real exchange rate has risen or is unchanged. As real exchange rates around the world change, the business is in a position to pursue market and production opportunities as they arise.

For example, suppose the value of the deutsche mark increases relative to the dollar faster than differences in German and American inflation rates would suggest with respect to purchasing power parity. A multinational corporation with production and marketing facilities in both countries would reduce production in Germany and increase production in America. Excess American production would be exported to Germany for sale in deutsche marks. The deutsche mark revenues would be converted to more dollars at the higher exchange rate.

A well-diversified multinational constantly encounters such opportunities for increased profits as a result of random fluctuations in real exchange rates. This serves to lower average costs and to raise average revenues over the long run, giving such companies a distinct competitive advantage.

Financing Strategies

Companies can also reduce economic exposure by matching assets and liabilities with respect to both currencies and maturities. (They should take care to match in terms of market values of assets and liabilities rather than book value.)

For example, an American company with a French subsidiary should attempt to finance the subsidiary with French franc denominated liabilities. These liabilities should have maturities similar to the lifetime of the subsidiary's assets. Hence, when the value of the franc decreases the dollar value of the subsidiary's assets, it will decrease the dollar value of the subsidiary's liabilities by a similar amount.

CHAPTER PERSPECTIVE

Economic exposure refers to changes in the market or economic value of a company that result from changes in currency values. To the extent that transaction and translation exposure affect the market value of the company, they are included in economic exposure. Multinational corporations, import/export businesses, and even some purely domestic operations are subject to economic exposure.

Economic exposure can be estimated by regressing past prices of a company's stock on past exchange rates for various currencies. The regression coefficients, which specify the change in the value of the stock for a unit change in the value of a particular currency constitute linear estimates of the company's economic exposure to that particular currency.

Techniques for reducing economic exposure include matching the currencies of cash inflows and outflows, diversification, and using strategic financing arrangements. It is impossible to hedge a company's economic exposure precisely because it is impossible to measure the factors that relate exchange rate changes to the company's market value precisely.

Financing Imports and Exports

INTRODUCTION AND MAIN POINTS

This chapter is the first of several to address specific areas of international corporate financial management. We begin by exploring international credit risk and the techniques available for controlling and managing it. Later chapters address international working capital management, capital budgeting, and long-term financing. These topics are primarily of interest to multinational corporations. However, international credit risk is also of great importance to domestic companies that are involved in importing and/or exporting.

After studying the material in this chapter:

— You will understand the special characteristics that distinguish international from domestic credit risk management.

— You will understand the function and operation of the letter of credit system.

— You will understand the basic contracts that are used to manage credit risk, such as bills of exchange, banker's acceptances, and shipping documents.

— You will understand the nature and purpose of forfaiting.

— You will be familiar with quasi-government institutions that help businesses control credit risk, such as the Import-Export Bank, the Foreign Credit Insurance Association, and the Private Export Funding Corporation.

INTERNATIONAL CREDIT RISK

Revenues on a company's income statement are matched to its expenses, which means that when revenue from an activity is recorded, all expenses associated with generating that revenue are deducted at the same time in order to determine profit. The actual cash flows associated with revenues and expenses almost never take place in the same period of time; payment for goods and services typically occurs several months after the order is placed and the goods delivered or services performed.

The difference in time between the origination of a sale, the delivery of the goods or services, and the actual flow of funds is reflected on the balance sheet in such items as accounts receivable, inventory, and accounts payable. When a business agrees to pay later for goods or services, its obligation is recorded as an accounts payable on its own balance sheet and as an accounts receivable on the supplier's balance sheet. When a company begins processing an order, raw materials, goods in process, and finished goods are recorded as inventory. If either party to the transaction fails to perform, these assets and liabilities are never paid and converted to cash; the profit recorded in one period becomes an offsetting loss in another period. The risk that one of the parties to the sale will fail to perform as promised is called *credit risk*; and all companies expend enormous resources, in some cases even forgoing profitable business, in order to control credit risk.

Credit risk in international business is complicated by a variety of factors. The time between the placement of orders and the flow of funds is greatly increased due to shipping and communications delays. Arrangements for extending credit are complicated by differences in legal systems and commercial cultures. Companies located in different countries are often unfamiliar with each other. The costs of enforcing agreements are increased and sometimes exceed the benefits. Uncertainties with respect to differences and changes in currency values and interest rates can create confusion and lead to disagreements and defaults.

The difficulties associated with business credit risk are so great that much mutually profitable commerce is lost. Even within the same country, credit risk is a serious problem. In the U.S., a major legal and regulatory effort has been made to induce the separate states to adopt a uniform commercial code. Despite major efforts of the United Nations and various organizations that seek to promote international economic development, there is no worldwide uniform commercial code.

THE LETTER OF CREDIT SYSTEM

Over the years, multinational banks have evolved a complex system for controlling credit risk and facilitating international commerce. This system is based upon a means of conducting international business transactions that is known as the *letter of credit*. A letter of credit can be used to transfer credit risk from the buyer and seller to the bank. Since multinational banks are regularly involved on a continuing basis in many transactions in many countries, they are able to develop expertise and economies of scale in international commercial transactions. They can then spread the benefits and costs over many transactions involving many companies.

The following sections explain how a simplified letter of credit system functions from the perspective of an American electronics retailer who imports from a Japanese manufacturer. After the basic system is described, we will present an overview of the system and some of the endless variations used throughout the world.

Applying for a Letter of Credit

Suppose a small American retailer wants to import and sell an electric motor produced by a small manufacturer in Japan. If the retailer were to contact the Japanese company, the Japanese producer would probably want payment in advance in yen, since it would want to avoid shipping on credit to an unknown company in a distant country where it would be too costly and time-consuming to collect in the event of default. The American retailer would not want to pay in advance, since small retailers have limited access to funds, and it would be too time-consuming and costly to enforce delivery if it never received the electric motors.

The solution to this dilemma is for a multinational bank that has offices in both the U.S. and Japan to guarantee the performance of both parties or, in other words, to assume the credit risk that would otherwise prevent the transaction. The process is initiated by the American retailer, who goes to the bank and applies for a letter of credit. If the bank issues the letter of credit, it assumes responsibility for the retailer's payment. Hence, it will do a detailed credit check and qualify the retailer just as it would before extending a short-term loan or a line of credit; sometimes the bank charges an application fee just as it would for some loans. The retailer must convince the bank that the business is profitable and legitimate.

If the bank determines that the application is for a legitimate and profitable purpose and that the retailer is creditworthy, it will approve the letter of credit application, issue the letter of credit, and so notify the Japanese manufacturer. The letter of credit will specify the type of product, the quantity and price, the means of delivery, and the terms of payment. The Japanese manufacturer now knows that if it ships goods on credit and complies with the terms of the letter of credit, it will receive payment as scheduled from the bank even if the American retailer defaults. In the event of a disagreement over terms, the manufacturer has to deal only with the bank in Japan under Japanese law and customs.

Shipping Documents

The American company can simply telex or fax its order to the Japanese manufacturer. The manufacturer assembles the order and delivers it to a shipping company in Japan. The shipper then prepares a bill of lading for the manufacturer. The *bill of lading* specifies the amount and condition of the goods, the destination, and in some cases conveys title to the goods.

The manufacturer or sometimes the shipper purchases shipping insurance and obtains any consular or commercial invoices, which are often necessary to allow shipment of some goods across international borders. Shipping insurance covers both intentional and accidental loss or damage during shipment.

Bills of Exchange

The Japanese company then presents the shipping documents, along with the letter of credit, to the Japanese branch of the multinational bank and draws a bill of exchange on the American company's account. *Bills of exchange* are typically called drafts and come in two basic varieties. *Sight drafts*, which are orders to pay a specified amount from a particular account on demand, are very similar to checks except that the signature of the account owner is not required; sometimes consumers allow mortgage companies or utilities to draw sight drafts on their checking accounts in order to avoid the time and expense of processing a bill and mailing a check. The bank will not accept the draft drawn by the exporter unless the Japanese manufacturer supplies the documents and complies with all conditions outlined in the letter of credit.

The second and more common variety of bill of exchange is a *time draft*. A time draft is an order to pay a specified amount from a particular account at some time in the future. It is similar to a postdated check except that the account owner's signature is not required. Most letters of credit require time drafts, which allow time for the goods to be received and sold before the funds must be deposited in the account to cover the draft.

Typically the exporter does not want to wait until the time draft matures in order to receive its funds. Hence, it usually discounts the time draft at the bank. *Discounting a draft* means that the bank purchases the time draft prior to maturity for an amount that is less than that specified on the time draft. This discount constitutes an implicit interest charge to the Japanese exporter for providing the funds prior to the maturity of the draft.

If the American importer defaults prior to maturity, the bank generally does not have recourse to the Japanese exporter. In cases where the exporter is a large creditworthy company, it may choose to offer the bank recourse in the event of default. In effect, the exporter guarantees the payment of the draft at maturity. This is usually done in order to induce the bank to charge a lower discount. The exporter guarantees the time draft by endorsing it, after which time it becomes known as a *trade acceptance*.

Banker's Acceptances

At any point in time, a large multinational bank holds billions of dollars' worth of discounted time drafts. Frequently banks wish to liquidate some of their discounted time drafts prior to maturity. They can do this by selling them to other banks, large corporations, or, in some cases, central banks. In order to facilitate the sale of the time drafts, banks always guarantee their payment at maturity regardless of the actions of the importer. A bank guarantees the discounted time draft by stamping its logo and endorsing it. Because the bank has now accepted recourse in the event of default, the endorsed and discounted time draft is called a *banker's acceptance*.

When a bank sells or discounts a time draft as a banker's acceptance, it receives more cash for it than it paid to the exporter, i.e., the discount is smaller. The bank is able to discount the banker's acceptance at a higher price because it is less risky and has a shorter term to maturity, since the bank typically holds it for a period of time before selling it. If the purchaser of the banker's acceptance is another bank, that bank may, after a period of time, also discount it. Usually, the second bank will also stamp, endorse, and guarantee payment. This process can go on through three and even four banks, each of which guarantees payment. Hence, banker's acceptances are some of the most risk-free money market instruments investors can buy.

An Overview

Figure 14-1 presents an overview of the operation of the basic letter of credit system. The major participants are the importer and the exporter, the multinational bank, the shipper, and the international money market, which represents other banks, large corporations, governments, and central banks.

The letter of credit system enables the importer and the exporter to conduct business as if they were dealing with companies in their respective countries. The bank acts like a Japanese company to the exporter and like an American company to the importer. Neither the importer nor the exporter has to be concerned with international credit risk since the performance of the other party is guaranteed by the bank.

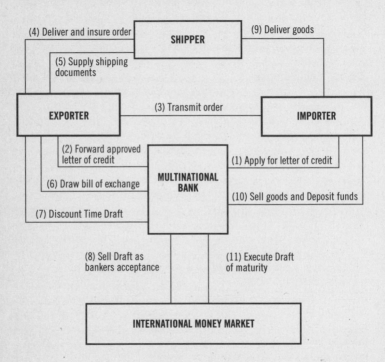

Fig. 14-1 *An overview of the letter of credit system*

The bank also allows the importer and the exporter to avoid many of the complexities of dealing in foreign currencies and capital markets. The importer can pay in dollars and calculate the benefits of deferred payment in U.S. rates of return. The exporter receives payment in yen and can calculate the cost of discounting in Japanese rates of return. The ability of the bank to discount the draft in the international money market assures an almost unlimited supply of funds to finance international commerce.

Variations on the Basic System

The procedures outlined in the previous sections were simplified in order to make it easier to understand the letter of credit system. In practice, there are many variations and complications. In this section, we explore some of the more common varieties of letters of credit.

In most situations, more than one bank is involved. The bank in the importer's country that receives and approves the letter of credit application is known as the *issuing bank*. If the issuing bank does not have offices in the exporter's country, it notifies either a correspondent bank in that country or the exporter's bank, which is known as the accepting bank. The *accepting bank* acts on behalf of the issuing bank but does not guarantee payment unless it specifically confirms the letter of credit for a fee.

Letters of credit may be *revocable* or *irrevocable*. An irrevocable letter of credit guarantees the exporter payment for performing its obligations even in the event that the importer wishes to withdraw from the transaction. Hence, an exporter who is preparing a special order for which there would likely be no other buyer would prefer an irrevocable letter of credit. *Revocable letters of credit* allow the importer to cancel the order prior to delivery of the shipping documents to the issuing bank (or to the accepting bank, if the letter of credit is confirmed). Once the appropriate documents have been presented, however, the bank must honor the agreement to issue a draft and guarantee payment.

A *straight letter of credit* specifies the price and amount of the order. If the company prefers to allow repeated orders at prices and in amounts that vary over time, a *negotiated letter of credit* is appropriate. A negotiated letter of credit allows for repeated orders at prices, in amounts, and for exchange rates that are negotiated at the time of the order. Very large and creditworthy importers may even allow a letter of credit to be transferable, in which case a wide variety of exporters may fill orders and draw bills of exchange for payment.

ALTERNATIVES TO THE LETTER OF CREDIT

In some situations a bank may be unwilling or unable to issue a letter of credit. These situations may involve importers located in underdeveloped countries or in countries with nonmarket economies and projects requiring the export of long-term capital such as factories, utilities, and transportation networks. A number of alternatives exist to facilitate trade and control credit risk.

Forfaiting

Forfaiting in some ways resembles a letter of credit arrangement for medium- or long-term financing of exports and imports. The process was inspired by the need of Eastern European countries to finance the import of capital equipment and sometimes entire manufacturing facilities. Because the currencies of these countries were often not convertible at market rates and government secrecy inhibited the free flow of information, a number of German, Swiss, and Austrian banks developed special subsidiaries, called forfaiters, to promote trade and provide financing for these projects.

Forfaiters finance foreign capital projects without recourse to the exporter, which means that the exporter need not worry about the creditworthiness of the importer. The term forfaiting is derived from a French term that means "to surrender a right," in this case the right of recourse against the exporter.

The first step is for the exporter and the importer to agree to a price and a schedule for completing and paying for the capital project. The exporter then contacts a forfaiter and negotiates a commitment to discount the importer's payments in the exporter's currency. Once the exporter, importer, and forfaiter agree to terms, formal contracts and promissory notes are prepared. The importer then has the notes endorsed (guaranteed) by the state bank and appropriate government agencies. The promissory notes are then delivered to the exporter, who discounts them with the forfaiter. The parent bank of the forfaiter can then endorse (guarantee) the notes in a manner similar to a banker's acceptance and sell them in the international money market.

Except for the long-term nature of the project and financing provided, forfaiting serves the same functions as the letter of credit system. The exporter is freed from credit risk, the importer obtains goods on credit, both avoid exchange rate risk, and the international money market provides unlimited credit.

GOVERNMENT GUARANTEES AND INSURANCE

In many cases governments have determined that there is a public interest in subsidizing exports. This public interest may range from providing jobs and protecting an export industry to assisting economic development in a less developed or socialist country. The U.S. government has developed a variety of institutions for stimulating exports when private self-interest fails to generate foreign trade.

The *Export-Import Bank* pursues three objectives on behalf of the United States. First, it guarantees loans to designated importers who purchase U.S. exports. Second, it provides direct loans in some cases. Third, it provides financial subsidies to help exporters compete against subsidized foreign competition.

The *Private Export Funding Corporation* (PEFCO) works with the Export-Import Bank to provide financing for medium- and long-term exports. PEFCO sells long-term bonds that are secured by Export-Import Bank guarantees and uses the proceeds to provide long-term financing for capital goods exports.

The *Foreign Credit Insurance Association* (FCIA) provides subsidized credit and political risk insurance to exporters. Banks can obtain insurance that allows them to confirm letters of credit from risky foreign banks and importers. It also insures bank leases for capital goods exports.

CHAPTER PERSPECTIVE

Importers and exporters are exposed to much greater levels of credit risk than are domestic businesses because of time delays, costly information, and great distances. The letter of credit system has evolved as an efficient system for lowering credit risk to importers and exporters while utilizing the economies of scale achieved by large multinational banks in providing credit evaluation, financing, and currency exchange.

In situations where the letter of credit is not feasible, business-es can resort to other methods. Forfaiting is useful for exporting large capital projects to countries with poorly developed or nonex-istent markets for credit and foreign exchange. In other situations, the purchase of credit insurance or outright government guarantees are useful.

Working Capital Management

INTRODUCTION AND MAIN POINTS

Chapters 15 and 16 explore financing options available to multi-national firms. Working capital management, the subject of this chapter, refers to the company's choices regarding current assets and current liabilities. Current asset and liability decisions are typically related to one another, since current assets are usually financed with current liabilities and often are used as collateral.

The focus in this chapter is on those techniques that distinguish multinational working capital management from purely domestic working capital management. With respect to cash management, we explore special remittance strategies and marketable securities. The discussion of receivables and payables focuses on factoring and countertrade. Inventory management techniques described include transfer pricing and advance repurchase. The discussion of short-term borrowing focuses on Euro-securities and floating rates.

After studying the material in this chapter:

■ You will understand the factors that complicate international working capital management.

■ You will be familiar with international business practices such as transfer pricing and countertrade.

■ You will be familiar with international money market instruments such as Eurodeposits, floating rate CDs, and the LIBOR.

■ You will understand the principles behind practices such as bilateral and multilateral netting.

CASH MANAGEMENT

Domestic corporate cash management strategies are designed to accelerate collections, lower transaction costs, minimize cash balances subject to liquidity constraints, and earn the highest possible rates of return on idle balances. In an international context, this is complicated by the costs of exchanging currencies, reducing transaction exposure, and avoiding controls on remittances. In the following two sections, we examine some remittance practices and marketable securities that are used by multinational companies.

Remittances

Many large multinational corporations centralize their international cash flow operations in a *centralized depository*. All affiliates and subsidiaries of the corporation make their international cash transactions with and through the centralized depository. These depositories are typically located in a large international money center such as London or New York but may be located anywhere if certain requirements, such as freedom of currency exchange, good communications, competitive international banking, minimal taxation, and well-defined, stable commercial laws are met. Centralization avoids duplication of effort and provides economies of scale with respect to human expertise and physical assets.

A major advantage of a centralized depository is that it facilitates the practice of *multilateral netting*. Bilateral netting between affiliates is simple to explain. For example, a British subsidiary of an American company may need to make three payments to the parent company and the parent company may need to make two payments to the subsidiary. The costs of exchanging currencies that result from different bid/ask rates and the bank charge for international fund transfers can be reduced if all five transactions are *netted* into one cash flow rather than five. Multilateral netting refers to the same strategy applied to more than two affiliates.

Some major industrialized countries such as France and Italy prohibit or restrict bilateral and multilateral netting of international cash flows. The purpose of these restrictions is to subsidize national banking systems by increasing the volume of international cash flows through the banking system.

Marketable Securities

The use of centralized depositories can also facilitate efforts to earn the highest available rates of return on idle cash balances. A central depository of a large multinational located in London may have bank balances denominated in several currencies. *Eurocurrencies* (sometimes called Eurodeposits) are bank deposits in one country that are denominated in the currency of another country.

For example, a dollar-denominated deposit in London, Brussels, or Frankfurt is called a Eurodollar. A deutsche mark-denominated deposit in London or New York is called a Euromark. Although dollar-denominated deposits in Tokyo, Singapore, or Hong Kong are often referred to as Asiadollars, they are also included in the definition of Eurocurrencies. Using a central depository, a company can convert to the currency of its choice and earn the corresponding Eurodeposit rate.

Eurodeposits can be made in a variety of maturities, from overnight in the interbank market up to a year. Companies may also choose to invest in floating-rate notes, sometimes called floating-rate CDs. *Floating-rate CDs* mature over an extended period of time but feature an interest rate that is periodically readjusted. Typically the interest rate is tied to the London Interbank Offer Rate (LIBOR) or the U.S. money market rate.

LIBOR is the interbank rate on Eurodollar deposits. Banks buy and sell short-term deposits in various currencies. Defaults are almost unheard of, so the LIBOR is very close to a risk-free borrowing and lending rate. Floating-rate loans and deposits are often quoted in terms of basis points above LIBOR. A basis point is 1/100 of a percent.

For example, a six-month floating-rate CD may pay 10 basis points above the one-month LIBOR rate, which means that each month the investor receives one-tenth of one percent more than the current LIBOR rate at the start of the month.

RECEIVABLES AND PAYABLES

When a company agrees to receive payment for goods and services at a later date, the amount owed is recorded as a payable account for the company that owes the money and a receivable account for the company that will receive the money. For purely domestic businesses, the management of payables and receivables revolves around a trade-off between the cost of payables to the customer as a form of financing and the increased sales by the supplier that result from receivables.

For multinational corporations, these decisions are complicated by changes in currency values and the possibility of restrictions on future remittances. The following sections describe some tools that facilitate the management of receivables and payables in international business.

Factoring

For small or irregular credit transactions, the letter of credit system is the preferred means of financing. For large or regular transactions, companies may wish to avoid the costs and involvement of a letter of credit arrangement. Receivables can be used as collateral for obtaining a bank loan, but the outright sale of foreign receivables is less risky and often less costly. The sale of a receivable is called *factoring*.

Factoring international receivables is more costly and risky to the factor than is purchasing domestic receivables. Hence, factors typically charge a higher discount and often refuse to factor receivables in amounts of less than $500,000. Factoring can be done with or without recourse. *Factoring with recourse* means that in the event of default the factor can recover the loss from the company that sold the receivable. Companies usually factor their international receivables without recourse.

Countertrade

Foreign trade with less developed countries often exposes the seller to enormous credit risks, since currencies are frequently regulated at unrealistic values and foreign remittances are subject to frequent restrictions and sometimes outright blocking. In addition, price controls and rationing frequently occur in these countries. *Countertrade* refers to a variety of mechanisms that are available to reduce these risks. All of the techniques that are referred to as countertrade include some form of reverse sale or transfer of goods.

The simplest form of countertrade is *barter*. In barter, sales are made and paid for by an exchange of goods; for example, 1000 tons of Polish coal for 100 tons of French cheese. In cases where the exchange cannot take place simultaneously, *bilateral clearing arrangements* can be made. The sale of the French cheese would earn a clearing balance with some government agency in Poland, and subsequent purchases of Polish coal would be paid from the clearing balance.

In some cases, clearing balances may be used to purchase a wide variety of goods. If the clearing balances are transferable, they may be purchased by *switch traders*, who purchase clearing balances at a discount and use them to purchase goods that they are then free to resell to anyone. Switch trading makes it possible to earn hard currency from the sale of goods and services to soft- or blocked-currency countries. For example, the French cheese exporter could sell its clearing balance in Poland to a German switch trader for deutsche marks.

Buyback or *compensation agreements* are another form of countertrade. In a buyback arrangement, an exporter of capital goods agrees to be compensated in the form of goods that are produced with the capital equipment. For example, an American chemical company may build a petrochemical complex in Russia in return for chemicals produced at the plant with Russian labor and petroleum. If the compensation agreement specifies compensation in the form of products unrelated to the capital good, the agreement is referred to as a counterpurchase.

The most flexible form of countertrade is known as an *offset*. Offsets specify that a product is to be assembled with some locally produced components. Offsets are used by many industrialized nations, particularly in the defense industry. For example, Japan may purchase U.S. fighter aircraft but specify that particular subassemblies and components must be produced in Japan.

INVENTORY MANAGEMENT

In a purely domestic business, inventory management consists of adding inventory until the rising marginal cost of holding additional inventory is offset by the falling marginal benefit of additional inventory. In an international context, this strategy is complicated by exchange rate fluctuations, price controls, restrictions on remittances, taxes, quotas, tariffs, and potential interference in the free flow of goods and services. The following sections describe some techniques for dealing with these complications.

Advance Purchase and Stockpiling

Prices of raw materials and supplies can be controlled in industrialized countries by using futures contracts and options. In other countries, companies often rely on advance purchases and stockpiling. These techniques have the added advantage of insulating the company from the effects of cutoffs and rationing.

If the company's supplies or finished goods are subject to quotas, inventory management can alleviate some of the effects. The business can increase inventories of imported finished goods in slow sales periods and reduce inventories in high sales periods. Raw materials can be stockpiled in slow periods and run down in expansions. These same techniques can be used to reduce the effect of, or take advantage of, changes in quotas and tariffs.

Transfer Pricing

The effects of restrictions on remittances and differences in corporate income taxes can be alleviated by careful use of transfer pricing. *Transfer pricing* refers to the cost one subsidiary or foreign affiliate charges another for a product transferred between them.

For example, suppose Brazil imposes a limit on the amount of corporate profit that a subsidiary can repatriate to its American parent. If the parent is shipping raw materials, components, or finished goods to the Brazilian subsidiary for assembly and sale, the subsidiary must record a cost in cruzeiros for these supplies. Profits earned by the subsidiary in Brazil depend on the transfer price charged to the subsidiary. In this case, the transfer price for materials produced in the U.S. can be raised. The profit in Brazil will be reduced, while the profit in the U.S. will be increased.

This transfer pricing strategy can also be applied to noninventory items. For example, royalties paid by the Brazilian subsidiary to the American parent for the use of technology can be increased. Charges to the Brazilian subsidiary for central management and administration can also be increased. All of the changes serve to increase profits recorded in the U.S. and reduce profits recorded in Brazil.

Free-trade Zones

Taxes and tariffs also influence inventory policy. Most modern industrialized nations have created *free-trade zones* that enable companies to import finished goods and materials into a country for assembly and distribution while deferring import duties and taxes. Businesses can use free-trade zones to stockpile inventory without giving up the option of later export should market conditions warrant it. Hence, free-trade zones defer costs and provide a ready means of mitigating the effects of price freezes and quotas.

SHORT-TERM BORROWING

For the most part, multinationals obtain short-term financing in the same way as do other businesses. They discount or factor their accounts receivable, they obtain line-of-credit agreements from banks, and they use their inventory as collateral to obtain short-term financing from financial institutions. Multinationals can denominate these loans in any currency and hedge their exposure but usually rely on the dollar. The following sections describe some of the special short-term borrowing arrangements used by some multinational firms.

Euronotes and Euro Commercial Paper

Euronotes are short-term notes issued by multinationals and sold in countries other than the one in whose currency they are denominated. They carry maturities of from one to six months and are most often denominated in dollars. Their interest rates are usually tied to the LIBOR.

Multinational banks act as underwriters for Euronotes, guaranteeing their sale and price. The banks spread the risk of large issues through underwriting syndicates.

Some of the largest and most creditworthy multinationals issue their Euronotes directly and avoid the expense of bank underwriting. Because these Euronotes are typically sold by commercial paper dealers, they are known as *Euro Commercial Paper.*

Fronting Loans

When a parent company provides short-term financing for a subsidiary in a developing country, it bears the risk that the developing country may impose restrictions on remittances and prevent future repayment. *Fronting loans*, which are sometimes refered to as *link financing,* are a means of reducing this risk.

Link financing involves the use of a financial intermediary outside the country of the parent company. Instead of making the loan directly, the parent deposits the amount of funds intended in the financial institution of a country that has good relations with the developing country. That financial institution then makes a loan to the subsidiary. Since interference in remittances to the financial institution of a friendly nation is less likely, the subsidiary is permitted to repay at maturity and the financial institution then returns the deposit to the parent.

CHAPTER PERSPECTIVE

For the most part, working capital management of multinationals is similar to working capital management of purely domestic companies. However, there are some special tools and techniques that are used to manage some of the special problems and risks that multinationals face.

Centralized methods of cash management assist multinationals in reducing the transaction costs associated with currency exchange and international fund transfers. Some special forms of marketable securities have evolved to facilitate the investment of idle funds and access to short-term credit. A wide variety of techniques known as countertrades are used to manage payable and receivable accounts in countries where currency values and convertibility are uncertain.

Long-term Financing

INTRODUCTION AND MAIN POINTS

In Chapter 15, we explored short-term financing arrangements of multinational companies in the context of working capital management. This chapter explains the major instruments and methods used by multinational companies to obtain long-term financing.

We begin by exploring some forms of medium-term financing that are popular in Europe and then explain some of the special features of international leasing. The many varieties of long-term bonds used in multinational finance are also described. The chapter concludes with a brief description of some of the advantages and disadvantages of international equity financing.

After studying the material in this chapter:

- You will be familiar with the use of medium-term debt instruments such as renewable overdrafts, bridge loans, and Euro-medium-term notes.
- You will understand the function of RURs, NIFs, and SNIFs.
- You will understand the special characteristics of international bonds such as foreign bonds, Eurobonds, currency cocktails, and dual-currency bonds.
- You will understand the complications that arise in international leasing and equity finance.

MEDIUM-TERM FINANCING

Medium-term financing refers to loans with a maturity of between one and 10 years. This type of financing is more popular in Europe than in the U.S. The following sections describe some of the more popular varieties of medium-term financing that are currently used by multinationals.

Renewable Overdrafts and Bridge Loans

Renewable overdrafts are widely used in Europe. They are very similar to a revolving line of credit as used in the U.S. Banks issue renewable overdrafts to companies contingent on their maintaining creditworthy status. Unlike a line of credit, renewable overdrafts are not paid down annually but are used as multi-year sources of funds.

Sometimes renewable overdrafts are used as temporary sources of funds prior to obtaining permanent long-term financing on capital projects. These are called *bridge loans.* Once the project is complete, the proceeds from the sale of long-term bonds that are collaterized by the project are used to pay off the bridge loan.

Euronote Rollovers

In the last chapter, Euronotes were described as a source of short-term funds similar to commercial paper but underwritten by banks. Euronotes can also serve as a medium-term source of funds if they are rolled over at maturity.

The risk that the company will not be able to sell new Euronotes to pay off the old ones as they mature can be eliminated by having a syndicate of banks guarantee in advance that subsequent Euronote issues will be purchased over a specific number of years.

Several types of syndicates have evolved to underwrite this risk. These include *Revolving Underwriting Facilities* (RUFs), *Note Issuance Facilities* (NIFs), and *Standby Note Issuance Facilities* (SNIFs). Despite minor differences in arrangements, all of these serve the common purpose of guaranteeing the sale of future Euronotes for the purpose of retiring each Euronote issue as it matures.

Euro-Medium-Term Notes

An alternative to rolling over Euronotes is the issuance of *Euro-medium-term* notes. These have maturities that range from one to 10 years, pay coupon interest, and feature fixed indentures that specify restrictive covenants and obligations of the borrower. They are sold directly to financial institutions on a continuing basis and avoid the cost of underwriting.

LEASING

In principle, international leasing arrangements should be no different from purely domestic leasing arrangements. However, due to differences in national tax policies and political risks, international leasing has developed special characteristics.

There are two major types of leases for tax purposes. *Financial leases* are permanent noncancellable financing arrangements that provide companies exclusive use of an asset over its entire economic lifetime. *Operating leases* are temporary and allow many companies partial use of an asset over its lifetime.

In some major countries, such as the U.S., Japan, and Germany, financial leases are recognized as a means of financing the ownership of an asset. Hence, they allow the company leasing the asset to take advantage of tax breaks such as depreciation and investment tax credits, even though formal ownership of the asset still resides with the company that is leasing the asset to them. In other countries, such as Britain, France, and Switzerland, the lessor is recognized as the owner and is entitled to these tax breaks.

Multinational companies can arrange leases among companies in different countries so that both the lessor and the lessee are granted the same tax breaks. For example, an American company can lease an aircraft from a French company on a permanent and noncancellable basis. Since the French company is getting the tax breaks in France, it will charge a lower fee. Since the Internal Revenue Service (IRS) considers the American company the economic owner, the IRS also allows them to take advantage of the same tax breaks. This arrangement is sometimes called double dipping.

Another advantage of international leasing is that it can reduce political risk. For example, an American company can provide equipment to Iranians by selling it to a Syrian leasing subsidiary, which in turn leases it to the Iranians. The Iranian government is less likely to take actions detrimental to a Syrian company than it is if an American company is affected.

Leases can also provide access to long-term capital in markets that are otherwise restricted to foreign businesses. For example, Japan severely limits the access of foreign companies to long-term bank loans in Japan. However, foreign companies can obtain long-term financial leases, sometimes called *Shogun leases*, from Japanese banks for the purchase of capital goods such as ships.

LONG-TERM DEBT FINANCING

Long-term debt financing in international markets is not restricted to multinational companies, although they are the predominant participants. In many cases, international bonds provide as many benefits to domestic businesses. Although bonds traded in the international market exhibit many of the attributes of ordinary bonds, they offer a variety of interesting and useful innovations. The following sections describe most of the more popular innovations.

Foreign Bonds

Foreign bonds are simply bonds sold outside the issuer's country. For example, an American corporation might sell bonds denominated in yen in Japan, which are sometimes called *Samurai bonds*. *Yankee bonds* are bonds issued by companies based outside the U.S., denominated in dollars and sold in the U.S. Bonds denominated in pounds and sold by foreign firms in Britain are sometimes called *Bulldog bonds*.

Although foreign bonds allow corporations to attract investors in foreign capital markets, they have some disadvantages. Because they are denominated in a foreign currency, they expose the business to exchange rate risk. Foreign bonds are also subject to regulatory restrictions in the country in which they are issued. Foreign bonds sold in the U.S. must comply with strict American disclosure requirements.

Eurobonds

Eurobonds may be issued by foreign or domestic companies but are denominated in a foreign currency. For example, a bond that is denominated in deutsche marks constitutes a Eurobond if it is sold outside Germany regardless of whether it is issued by a business based in Germany or elsewhere. Most Eurobonds are denominated in dollars and sold in Europe, in many cases to Organization of Petroleum Exporting Countries (OPEC) investors who receive their oil payments in dollars. In recent years there has been a rapid growth in nondollar denominated Eurobonds; many dollar-denominated Eurobond issuers are American companies.

Large syndicates of multinational banks typically underwrite new Eurobond issues. Part of the appeal of Eurobonds is that they are subject to few national regulations. Primary and secondary markets for Eurobonds are subject to voluntary regulation by the *Association of International Bond Dealers*. Because of the minimal regulation, only the largest and most creditworthy businesses can participate in the Eurobond market.

The absence of controls extends to matters of taxation. Eurobonds are *bearer bonds*, meaning they are not registered and taxes are not withheld on interest income earned. Many Eurobonds are held in Swiss accounts by non-Swiss investors. Unless the interest is voluntarily declared, it is tax-free. The attractiveness of this feature was reduced in the 1980s when the U.S. government also began issuing bearer bonds in Europe.

Eurobonds can feature fixed interest rates or floating interest rates. *Floating-rate Eurobonds* provide coupon interest payments that are tied to the LIBOR. The rate of interest may be adjusted annually or semiannually. By the mid-1980s most Eurobonds carried floating interest rates rather than fixed rates.

Recently, some Eurobonds have featured the option of conversion into a fixed number of shares of the issuing company's stock. Convertible bonds have long been featured in the domestic market; convertible Eurobonds are known as *equity-related issues*.

Currency Cocktails

Whether a company issues foreign bonds or Eurobonds, the bonds are subject to fluctuations in the value of the currency in which they are denominated. This risk can be reduced by denominating the bond in units of some average of a basket of currencies; these types of bonds are often referred to as currency cocktails.

Currency cocktails can be denominated in any combination of any number of currencies. However, most are denominated in terms of *Special Drawing Rights* (SDRs) or *European Currency Units* (ECUs). SDRs are issued by the International Monetary Fund and were originally tied to the value of gold. In the 1970s their value was set equal to a weighted average of 16 major currencies whose weights were determined by the country's percent of world trade. In the 1980s the formula was changed again; the value of an SDR is now a weighted average of the dollar, the pound, the yen, the deutsche mark, and the franc. The highest weight is given to the dollar, followed by the yen and deutsche mark.

Most currency cocktails are denominated in ECUs. The ECU is a weighted average of the currencies of countries in the European Monetary Union, which does not include Britain. The value of ECUs are currently most closely related to the value of the deutsche mark. In recent years, a growing number of European businesses have denominated their bonds in ECUs, and ECU-denominated bonds now outnumber bonds denominated in some major currencies, such as the Dutch guilder. This trend is likely to accelerate as a consequence of European economic union in 1992.

Dual-Currency Bonds

Some Eurobonds, called *dual-currency bonds,* offer investors the option of receiving interest and principle payments in either of two currencies. Investors benefit by being able to choose compensation in the currency that has appreciated the most. This option is costly to the issuer; however, issuers are able to sell these bonds at lower rates.

Some dual-currency bonds specify that interest is to be paid in one currency and principal in another. These bonds do not offer the investor the option of choosing the currency. Although this provision is advantageous to some companies, there are few advantages to the investor; hence, companies are not able to issue them at lower rates.

Indexed Bonds

Indexed bonds are bonds that feature interest and principal payments tied to the value of a commodity or some other identifiable index. Most indexed bonds are tied to the value of gold or some other tradable commodity. Some companies have issued Eurobonds that feature payments indexed to some measure of performance, such as revenues or profits. One resort company issued Eurobonds tied to the room charges and occupancy rates of its resorts.

EQUITY FINANCING

In recent decades some multinational corporations have begun to issue their stock in several countries. In order to provide a market for the issue, they also list company stock on several exchanges in different countries. Some companies have even simultaneously syndicated new issues on several different national exchanges.

There are substantial costs associated with listing on overseas exchanges. First, exchanges often charge a substantial listing fee. Second, foreign governments and the exchanges themselves compel the company to disclose substantial amounts of information that often must be audited and certified by outside consultants. Third, a major effort must be made to educate foreign press, brokers, and potential investors about the nature and prospects of the company.

The benefits of foreign listing are more intangible. If stock is seen as a commodity, then foreign listings make it available to more customers (investors). If the company has a subsidiary in a foreign country, then listing in that country may improve government relations and promote a sense of local participation in the development of the business. Studies of foreign listings for U.S.-based multinationals have not shown measurable benefits. The benefits to foreign companies based in small countries with poorly developed capital markets may be more substantial, but there are few examples.

CHAPTER PERSPECTIVE

International capital markets offer a variety of innovative long-term financing arrangements for multinational firms. For medium-term financing, companies can utilize renewable overdrafts, Euro-medium-term notes, and various underwritten rollover strategies for Euronotes. International leasing provides several advantages for reducing corporate income taxes, penetrating restricted capital markets, and managing political risk.

A wide variety of Eurobonds that feature fixed or floating rates and a choice of currency denominations are available. Companies can even denominate their bonds in baskets of currencies such as SDRs or ECUs or index the bonds to gold, commodities, or performance measures. Potential investors can even be offered the option of choosing among several currencies when receiving payments of interest and principal. The opportunity to avoid both regulations and taxes makes the international bond markets appealing to many companies and investors. The advantages of international equity markets are more difficult to define, but many large multinationals use this avenue as well.

Managing Political Risk

INTRODUCTION AND MAIN POINTS

Companies that do business in foreign countries are subject to the laws and regulations of the particular country in which they operate. *Political risk* results from potential changes in a nation's laws and regulations. These changes can affect the value of foreign operations. International financial management includes measuring and controlling the effect of political changes on the business.

After studying the material in this chapter:

■ You will understand the nature and consequences of political risk.

■ You will be familiar with the basic techniques that can be used to measure the probability and quantify the magnitude of political risk.

■ You will be able to design methods for reducing political risk prior to making foreign investments.

■ You will understand a variety of operating policies that can be used to manage political risk.

■ You will know what alternatives are available to a company that is the victim of foreign political action.

NATURE AND CONSEQUENCES OF POLITICAL RISK

At the mention of political risk, many American managers think of a left-wing, bearded, Latin American dressed in army fatigues, smoking a cigar and railing against Yankee imperialists. While it is true that such characters are related, in a very minor way, to political risk, the actual impact of political risk is much more subtle and widespread. A more accurate picture of political risk would be a group of democratically elected legislators raising corporate taxes and passing new business regulations.

National governments are sovereign. They can regulate, tax, and control business and investment activity within their borders as they see fit. Although they are often subject to international treaties and multilateral agencies, they can break these obligations if they choose.

Political risk (sometimes called country or sovereign risk) refers to the consequences that companies must bear as a result of future changes in government policy. A country can have a very unfavorable attitude towards business but present very little political risk if it is unlikely to change policies in the future. Political risk refers only to *uncertainty* about, or variability in, government policies that affect businesses or investors. Political risk can also refer to quasigovernmental activities of unions, trade organizations, and the political opposition to a government. In the following sections, we examine some of the potential changes that can affect a company.

Expropriation and Nationalization
Expropriation and nationalization have the most direct impact on the value of a company. *Expropriation* refers to the seizure by a government of foreign businesses and assets within its own territory. Expropriation is always involuntary but often includes some form of compensation. If the compensation is satisfactory to the owners, then the seizure is voluntary and not considered expropriation.

Compensation may be, but is usually not, in the form of a marketable currency. Often compensation is in the form of a restricted currency that can be exchanged for marketable currencies only at highly unfavorable regulated exchange rates. Usually the owners are compensated in the form of government securities, such as bonds, that carry a very high par value but a very low or nonexistent interest rate. Frequently these securities are not marketable. In cases where they are, the market value is only a small fraction of par value. Almost all governments, including the U.S., have expropriated some foreign businesses and assets. Usually, however, expropriation is committed by the major industrial countries only during wartime.

Nationalization is similar to expropriation, but more frequently observed. *Nationalization* differs from expropriation in that it refers to seizure by the government of all companies, both foreign and domestic. Although some governments have nationalized all businesses, they usually nationalize a particular industry, such as banking or mining. In some cases, only large corporations, oligopolies, or monopolies are nationalized. Owners of nationalized companies are almost always compensated. In some cases, the compensation is satisfactory, and nationalization is tantamount to a market sale of the business or its assets. Such voluntary nationalizations are not the subject of political risk. Political risk is associated with the possibility of involuntary nationalization that entails below-market-value compensation.

Interference
Government interference in the conduct of business or the management of assets is much more common, and in many cases, more costly than either nationalization or expropriation. Interference can be overt, as in the case of formal regulations, licensing of activities, price controls, and rationing, or it can be covert, as in the case of bureaucratic delays, exaggerated inspections, violations of proprietary information, extortion of bribes, and litigation of phony accusations of improper conduct.

Interference may be directed specifically at foreign-owned business or at companies in general. In some cases, only particular industries or large companies are targeted. Examples include variations in fees for infrastructure services such as transportation, utilities, schools, and public health. Political risk is also associated with variations in the quality or quantity of services provided to a foreign-owned business. Sometimes public-sector infrastructure investments can be targeted to give a competitive advantage to domestic companies, while foreign businesses suffer from intermittent interruptions in telephone, gas, and electric service.

Interference is often directed at the financial operations of the company. For example, domestic competitors may be allowed to borrow at subsidized rates, or foreign businesses may be denied access to domestic banking services. Restrictions may be placed upon remittances in the form of dividends and interest to foreign owners. Foreign companies may be forced to convert foreign funds at unfavorable exchange rates. Often foreign businesses are required to reinvest earnings in the domestic economy. Sale of equity in foreign businesses can be restricted to domestic companies and to individuals.

Sometimes the source of interference is outside the government. Unions can go on strike or engage in work slowdowns over issues unrelated to employment. Consumer groups can engage in boycotts or lockouts. Political groups can stage riots, insurrections, and sabotage. Trade groups and intermediaries may show favoritism toward domestic businesses. Some groups and institutions may engage in legal and regulatory harassment by filing false claims involving health and safety violations, environmental damage, and product liability.

The goals of these types of interference vary. Sometimes the purpose is to give domestic companies a competitive advantage. At other times, the purpose can be to reduce the foreign company's market value so that another party can purchase it at a reduced price. Often interference is directed at extorting some concession from the company. Whatever the goal, the effect is a reduction in the value of the business.

Taxation

A major source of political risk is the potential for future changes in taxation. These tax changes can be directed at either corporate income, revenues, or personal income. Corporate income taxes can be altered by changing tax rates, deductions, credits, or accounting rules for computing income. Corporate revenue taxes such as the value-added tax, sales tax, excise tax, and tariffs can be changed by varying either the rates or the coverages. Personal taxes on the income of foreign business owners and assets can be changed by varying the tax rates or computing of income by modifying rules on captital gains and deductability of interest.

For the majority of the major industrial powers, potential future changes in taxation constitute the dominant source of political risk. In the U.S., proposals for major changes in the tax code that affect businesses and investors are fought over every year. The situation is no different in Japan, Germany, Britain, France, and the other major powers. Changes in tax laws can have a greater effect on the value of firms than more publicized and dramatic actions such as expropriation or nationalization. Because the probability of tax changes is so much greater, it constitutes the source of most political risk.

MEASURING POLITICAL RISK

Because political risk relates to events that take place in the future, there is no precise way to measure it. Domestic businesses can ignore it to the extent that it is unavoidable and must be borne. However, multinational corporations must attempt to measure differences in political risk among different countries if they are to optimize their operations. No one method of measuring political risk is appropriate for all businesses and all countries. In the following sections, we review some of the more widely used techniques for measuring political risk.

Political risk is best assessed at both the macro and the micro level. *Macro-level assessment* is directed at evaluating the political risk of the country in relation to other countries. *Micro-level assessment* is concerned with evaluating political risk in a particular country with respect to particular industries or companies.

For example, companies that are engaged in extracting irreplaceable mineral resources bear a much greater degree of political risk than do those engaged in high-tech manufacturing. Nations have less to gain in the future from industries that extract a nonrenewable resource than they do from industries that develop technology and human capital. Similarly, businesses that are identified with a particular country are more exposed than are those that have a truly multinational character.

Subjective Methods

There are two basic approaches to making subjective estimates of political risk for a particular country. The first is sometimes referred to as a grand tour. Grand tours consist of a visit to the country in question by the company's key executives and their assistants. They arrange to meet with as many government officials and community leaders as possible. Most countries have a special government department that specializes in attracting foreign investment.

The second variety of subjective assessments of political risk can be classified as Delphi techniques, a term derived from the Oracle at Delphi, who predicted the future for rulers and merchants in ancient times. Modern forecasters of political risk are usually consulting firms set up by former State Department officials and university experts. They prepare both micro and macro political risk assessments for corporations and charge substantial fees. Although there is no independent evidence relating to the reliability of these forecasts, they offer management a defense against angry stockholders if a company unexpectedly suffers the consequences of political risk.

Major business publications, including *The Wall Street Journal* and *Business Week,* publish rankings of countries' political risk. These rankings are based upon the subjective judgments of many experts. Each country is evaluated subjectively by the experts acting independently; the responses are then averaged and compiled for publication.

Quantitative Methods

Quantitative measures of political risk attempt to index a country relative to others with respect to political risk or to estimate the probability of a major loss being suffered. There are two types of quantitative measures of political risk. The first type of measure is purely statistical and is based upon historical correlations between certain measurable variables and subsequent losses related to political risk. The second type is based upon a socio-political-behavioral theory concerning the factors that lead to actions that result in losses from political risk.

Multiple discriminant analysis is an example of a purely statistical measure of political risk. It is a statistical procedure for identifying specific measurable socio-economic variables that are related to political actions that result in losses to foreign subsidiaries. They are identified from historical data. Once identified, the relevent variables are assigned weightings such that, when current observations of the present value of the variables are multiplied by these weights and added up, a *z-score* is obtained that can be converted into a probability that a loss will be suffered.

The *Political System Stability Index* is an example of a theoretically based system for measuring political risk. In order to avoid biased opinions and promote objectivity, the overall measure is composed of three subindices that reflect measures of societal conflict, government processes, and socio-economic characteristics of the society. These estimates also include a measure of the level of confidence in their accuracy.

MANAGING POLITICAL RISK

There is no way to eliminate or completely control political risk. However, companies can take steps and pursue policies that lower the probability of unfavorable political action and that reduce the magnitude of the consequences should such actions take place. Management of political risk begins prior to investment, continues during operations, and does not cease once unfavorable political action takes place.

Actions Prior to Investing

Prior to making a direct foreign investment in a country, management should try to ensure that the local government and citizenry understand both the costs and the benefits of the investment to both the company and the local community. Management should meet with government officials and citizen groups to clarify the goals of the business and its operational procedures. Political risk is largely mitigated to the extent that everyone's expectations about the costs and benefits of the investment are fulfilled. Political risk increases when local governments and/or the public are surprised by outcomes or developments.

A formal procedure for achieving this understanding is to negotiate a formal *concession agreement*. A concession agreement spells out the rights of the company and its obligations to the foreign host. For example, a concession agreement might spell out the owners' rights to remittances in the form of dividends, royalties, and administrative fees. It might also specify taxation of corporate income, tariffs on imports, and transfer prices. It might provide for access to local credit markets or planned divestment, which means the gradual transfer of ownership to local investors. Concession agreements can also specify the use of arbitration or mediation procedures for the resolution of disputes.

In summary, a concession agreement may specify any aspect of the company's relationship with the host country. However, a caveat is in order with respect to concession agreements—they are binding on the host country only to the extent that the government voluntarily complies. There is no enforcement for concession agreements violated by host governments.

Another strategy for controlling political risk is to obtain political risk insurance from a government agency such as the *Overseas Private Investment Corporation* (OPIC), which was set up by the U.S. government to provide political risk insurance for American companies making direct foreign investments.

OPIC offers four types of insurance coverage. First, it insures against restrictions on the remittance of income from the foreign subsidiary in the form of dollars. Second, it insures against expropriation and nationalization. Third, it insures against damage to assets from war, insurrection, and civil disturbances. Fourth, it insures against loss of business income that results from political conflict and disturbances.

Actions During Operations

After a foreign subsidiary has been established, there are a variety of methods that are still available for controlling political risk.

If a company controls the movement of raw materials and finished goods, a host country has little to gain from interfering in the company's operations. For example, if a subsidiary is seized and the parent company can shut off supplies of critical raw materials or components used in manufacture or operations, then the subsidiary cannot operate and must be shut down, with the consequent loss of jobs and income to the host country. Similarly, if the subsidiary is dependent upon the parent for marketing or to purchase its product, the parent can force it to cease operations following a seizure, again to the detriment of the host country.

Parent companies can also lessen the likelihood of seizure or interference by controlling access to evolving technologies or brand names and trademarks. For example, a subsidiary that produces microelectronics would soon be obsolete if it were to be isolated from new machinery or manufacturing processes. Sales of some products such as beverages are dependent on brand name or trademark recognition.

Finally, a parent can lessen its exposure to political risk by relying on local credit markets for expansion capital and by seeking the participation of local equity investors. Shared ownership agreements, along with gradually increasing transfers of equity to local investors, lessen the likelihood of political interference.

Actions Subsequent to Seizure

Strategies are available to managers even after political action has been taken against the company. For example, foreign owners can request that the government's political opposition or sometimes the governments of neighboring countries apply pressure to a host government. Economic sanctions can sometimes be applied by the government of the parent company.

Companies should not ignore legal remedies. Although the legal doctrines of sovereign immunity and acts of state limit the recourse to courts in other countries, foreign countries sometimes voluntarily submit disputes to the International Center for Settlement of Investment Disputes, which provides mediation or binding arbitration.

General Principles

Whenever companies deal with sovereign governments, their guiding principle should be mutual self-interest. Business arrangements should be conducted in a manner such that both the company and the host country continue to obtain benefits that would not be available if the relationship were to end. Companies should avoid situations where they provide benefits to the host country up front and then expect to obtain future benefits to the detriment of the host country. Governments generally find a means of ending arrangements that no longer provide benefits to their citizens.

This principle should be familiar to most businesses, since it also guides their relationships with domestic customers, suppliers, and employees. Any of these parties are free to interrupt their relationship with the business. They choose not to only if the relationship is mutually beneficial and is in their own self-interest.

CHAPTER PERSPECTIVE

Political risk refers to potential losses that can result from actions taken against the company's interest by governments and groups within a host country. All companies are exposed to some degree of political risk regardless of where their operations are located; American businesses are exposed to substantial levels of political risk in the U.S., since income taxes and regulations are always subject to change.

Well-managed companies expend resources measuring and managing political risk. Where political risk levels are high, companies can avoid making investments or can attempt to establish mutually beneficial, continuing relationships. If management recognizes that others usually act in their own self-interest and is willing to pursue activities that offer benefits to others, then political risk can be effectively controlled.

Direct Foreign Investment

INTRODUCTION AND MAIN POINTS

Direct foreign investment refers to the ownership of real assets, such as factories, machinery, and real estate. Investment in financial assets such as stocks and bonds is discussed in Chapter 20. Sometimes the distinction between investment in real and financial assets is blurred, as in the case of an acquisition of an existing foreign subsidiary. Such cases are addressed in this chapter.

We begin the study of direct foreign investment with a discussion of the motives behind it. The basic techniques of direct foreign investment are then described. We conclude with an examination of how the desirability of direct foreign investment is evaluated.

After studying the material in this chapter:
- You will understand the basic political, economic, and competitive factors that influence direct foreign investment.
- You will be familiar with the most frequently used methods of making direct foreign investments.
- You will understand the factors that distinguish capital budgeting decisions regarding foreign investment.
- You will be able to estimate the value of proposed direct foreign investments.

MOTIVES FOR DIRECT FOREIGN INVESTMENT

The simplest way of earning a return on investment in a foreign country is to purchase financial assets such as stocks and bonds in a foreign company. The next simplest alternative is either to export to a foreign country or license a foreign company. These alternatives allow a company to avoid the risks and expenses associated with transferring personnel, dealing with foreign languages and cultures, obtaining supplies, developing markets, operating in foreign political environments, and a host of other problems.

Nevertheless, many of the world's most successful companies find it in the interest of their investors to incur these risks and expenses by making direct foreign investments. In the following sections we explore the political, economic, and competitive motives behind direct foreign investment.

Political Motives

Some of the most obvious motives for direct foreign investment are political. Governments are frequently convinced that it is in their best interest to deny or restrict their citizens access to goods and services from abroad. Despite the clear disadvantages of denying consumers foreign goods that are better made and/or less expensive, governments often act out of a desire to protect domestic jobs from perceived threats or out of nationalism and/or xenophobia.

Foreign businesses that are denied the right to export to a country often find that they can penetrate the market by agreeing to manufacture or at least assemble goods within the target country. Sometimes these same tactics are used to overcome restrictions on imports such as quotas, tariffs, and import duties. Local production mitigates concerns about job loss and nationalistic pride.

Political motives for direct foreign investment are not always related to overcoming restrictions on trade. Sometimes political factors are used by local authorities as inducements. Parent organizations that are located in countries where increased taxation, regulation, and/or other forms of interference are present or threatened can avoid these problems by transferring operations to countries that will treat them more favorably. A truly multinational business is usually less subject to unfavorable political action because local governments are constrained by the ability of the business to transfer operations elsewhere, costing the current host country jobs, revenues, and perhaps prestige.

Economic Motives

Economic factors can also motivate direct foreign investment. Some companies can obtain substantial economies of scale in areas such as research and development, marketing, distribution, financing, and production by operating at volumes that can be justified only by a worldwide market.

For example, the Swedish auto and aerospace markets are not large enough to spread the substantial investment required to develop advanced products. Swedish auto and aerospace companies are compelled to participate in multinational production and distribution. Companies in larger countries are able to spread these costs over a much larger sales volume.

In addition to economies of scale that are provided by multinational operations, companies can overcome shortages and imperfections in local markets for factors of production. Perhaps the local population cannot provide sufficient numbers of technicians and engineers, or particular raw materials may be unavailable or overpriced in local markets. Multinational production facilitates access to the factors of production at the lowest available cost.

As explained in Chapter 13, multinational corporations that produce and sell in many countries can exploit fluctuations in real exchange rates. When exchange rate changes raise inflation-adjusted prices in one country and lower them in another, the company can shift production to the low-cost country and sales to the high-price country.

Competitive Motives

Competitive motives for direct foreign investment are closely related to, and difficult to distinguish from, economic and political motives. A business may make direct foreign investments in cases where the immediate economic and/or political benefits are not clear. The motive is often related to securing the business against the threat of existing or potential competition.

For example, companies may seek to establish international market share or production even though the effort is apparently unprofitable, as in cases of dumping, or the export of products at prices that are below the cost of production. The purpose of such actions is often to undermine an existing or potential competitor. Once market share is established, production costs fall or prices are raised. In many cases, dumping constitutes an illegal activity punishable by fines and compensatory payments to companies that have been damaged.

In some cases, companies have lobbied for the establishment of protectionist barriers against foreign businesses in order to foster the development of a domestic industry that does not yet exist (known as "infant industry" policies).

Another example of competitively motivated direct foreign investment is a merger with or an acquisition of a foreign business for the purpose of gaining access to foreign technology. Sometimes investments are made in foreign companies in order to gain access to foreign marketing or production expertise. Many governments have established barriers to such acquisitions.

METHODS OF DIRECT FOREIGN INVESTMENT

The simplest method of direct foreign investment is the acquisition of or merger with an existing foreign business. If the company's securities are publicly traded, the risk of overpaying for the assets is lessened. An alternative approach is to engage in construction of real assets in a foreign country.

Businesses may attempt to lessen some of the uncertainty or political risk of direct foreign investment by seeking a partner. For example, they may engage in a joint venture with a foreign company in which both partners contribute capital and share ownership of a subsidiary. This subsidiary may be a previously existing company, or the partners may construct or import the real assets.

Sometimes companies will enter into an alliance with a foreign partner. These alliances can serve many purposes. They may cooperate in marketing in their respective countries; they may agree to share technology or engage in joint research and development projects; sometimes they license each other's products or production techniques. Alliances can be very informal or they can be spelled out contractually. In some cases, one of the partners makes an equity investment in the other, often for a special class of stock.

INTERNATIONAL CAPITAL BUDGETING

Capital budgeting is the procedure for evaluating and selecting investments in long-term real assets. The concept of *Net Present Value* (NPV) constitutes the theoretical framework within which capital budgeting is carried out. Readers who desire a more detailed presentation of the concept of net present value can refer to any introductory textbook on corporate financial management. In the following sections we review the application of NPV and relate it to international capital budgeting.

Net Present Value

A project's Net Present Value is the value of all present and future net cash flows, adjusted for the effects of risk and time. We define a net cash flow in period (Ct) as the sum of all cash inflows to the company in that time period minus the sum of all cash outflows from the company in that time period.

The effect of time on the value of cash flows is best understood by considering the effect of interest earned on cash deposits. A sum of cash deposited now, referred to as time period zero, is denoted as C_0. If left on deposit, it will earn interest equal to the amount of cash (C_0) times the interest rate (r):

$$C_0 + rC_0 = C_0(1 + r)$$

For a deposit of $100 and an interest rate of 10 percent, this equals

$$\$100 (1 + .10) = \$110$$

If the money is left on deposit for two years, it will earn an additional 10 percent on the $110 balance at the end of the first year:

$$\$110 (1 + .10) = \$121$$

If the money is left on deposit for a third year, it will earn an additional 10 percent on the $121 balance at the end of the second year,

$$\$121 (1 + .10) = \$133.10$$

The effect of time on the value of money is to multiply its value by $(1 + r)$ for each year. This is called *compounding*. The value of money left for t years is compounded, which means multiplied by $(1 + r)$, t times:

$$C_0(1 + r)(1 + r)...(1+ r) = C_0(1 + r)^t$$

For example, if the rate of return is 12 percent, the value of $2,000 in 10 years is

$$C_0(1 + r)^t = \$2000(1 + .12)^{10} = \$6211.70$$

Hence, if the rate of return is 12 percent, investors are indifferent to receiving $6211.70 in 10 years or $2,000 immediately. If given $2,000 today, they could deposit it and earn 12 percent for 10 years. If given $6211.70 in 10 years they could borrow $2,000 today, which would accumulate interest at 12 percent for 12 years until they received the money.

This principal of indifference allows us to calculate the present value of money received in the future. From the previous example, we know that

$$\$6211.70 = \$2000(1 + .12)^{10}$$

Therefore,

$$\$2,000 = \$6211.70/(1 + .12)^{10}$$

Expressed algebraically, the present value (V_0) of a net cash flow in period t (Ct) is

$$V_0 = C_t/(1 + r)^t .$$

In order to determine the Net Present Value of a project, we simply determine the present value of each period's net cash flow and then add them up:

$$NPV = C_0 + C_1/(1 + r)^1 + C_2/(1 + r)^2 +...+ C_n/(1 + r)^n$$

where n is the last or nth period. For example, consider a project that requires an outlay of $1 million today and that will return $700,000 in each of the next two years. Due to its risk, the company requires a 16 percent rate of return. The project's net present value is

$$\text{NPV} = -1,000,000 + 700,000/(1.16) + 700,000/(1.16)^2$$
$$= \$123,662.31$$

Hence, investing in this project will increase the value of the company by $123,662.31.

Value of Foreign Currency Cash Flows

When a company makes a direct foreign investment, it typically makes a current outlay in its home currency and receives future returns in foreign currency. This complicates the process of capital budgeting. The company must estimate the effect of all future changes in exchange rates on the home currency value of all future foreign currency cash flows.

Consider an American company that will receive a net cash flow in a foreign currency in time period t. We denote the cash flow as $_fC_t$ where the subscript f indicates that the cash flow is in foreign currency units. The dollar value of the foreign currency cash flow at time period t is equal to the foreign currency value times the value of the foreign currency in dollars at time t:

$$_sC_t = {_fC_t} \, (\$/f)_t$$

Since the present value of a dollar cash flow is

$$V_0 = C_t/(1 + r)^t$$

the present dollar value of the foreign currency cash flow is

$$_sV_0 = [_fC_t \, (\$/f)_t]/(1 + r)^t$$

For example, suppose the company expects to receive 100 million marks in five years. It requires a rate of return of 14 percent and expects the value of the mark to be $0.60 in five years. The present dollar value of this cash flow is

$$_sV_0 = [100 \text{ million } (0.60)]/(1.14)^5$$
$$= \$31,162,119.86$$

Unfortunately, the accuracy of this estimate depends upon the accuracy of the company's forecast of the value of the mark.

A company that wants to calculate the dollar Net Present Value of a foreign capital budgeting project must estimate the future dollar/mark exchange for every period over the life of the investment. The difficulty of making accurate exchange rate forecasts over extended periods of time can lead to large errors in estimates of the project's value. To the extent that the International Fisher Effect holds, however, this procedure can be simplified and made more accurate.

Recall that the International Fisher Effect relates changes in the future value of a currency to relative interest rates in the two countries:

$$(\$/f)_{t+1} = (\$/f)_t (1 + r_\$)/(1 + r_f)$$

Hence,

$$(\$/f)_1 = (\$/f)_0 (1 + r_\$)/(1 + r_f)$$

and

$$(\$/f)_2 = (\$/f)_1 (1 + r_\$)/(1 + r_f)$$

Therefore,

$$(\$/f)_2 = (\$/f)_0 (1 + r_\$)^2/(1 + r_f)^2$$

In general, the International Fisher Effect can relate the future value of the exchange rate in any period t to the present value of the exchange rate and relative interest rates by the following formula:

$$(\$/f)_t = (\$/f)_0 (1 + r_\$)^t/(1 + r_f)^t$$

For example, if the current value of the mark is \$0.55 and the 10-year interest rates in Germany and the U.S. are seven percent and nine percent, respectively, then the expected future value of the mark in 10 years is

$$(\$/M)^{10} = (0.55) (1.09)^{10}/(1.07)^{10}$$
$$= \$0.6612$$

If we substitute this formula for the expected future value of the exchange rate into our formula for the present dollar value of a future foreign currency cash flow, we obtain a simplified estimator for present dollar values,

$$_\$V_0 = [_fC_t (\$/f)_0]/(1 + r_f)^t$$

This estimator avoids the problem of estimating future exchange rate values and requires a knowledge only of the current exchange rate, $(\$/f)_0$, and the current foreign interest rate, which are both readily available.

For example, suppose the company expects to receive 200,000 marks in three years. We find out that the current value of the mark is $0.55 and that the five-year rate of return rate in Germany is eight percent. The present dollar value of this cash flow is

$$_\$C_0 = [200,000 \ (0.55) \ ]/(1.08)^3$$
$$= \$87,321.55$$

When a business estimates the Net Present Value for a project, it is not necessary to multiply each future foreign currency value by the current exchange rate. Since each cash flow in the sum is multiplied by the same exchange rate, the Net Present Value of the foreign currency can be estimated by using foreign currency values and foreign interest rates. Then the Net Present Value is simply multiplied by the exchange rate to get its dollar value:

$$NPV\$ = (\$/f)_0\{NPV_f\}$$

While it is true that the accuracy of these Net Present Value estimates depends upon the extent to which the International Fisher Effect holds, alternative methods that are based on obtaining forecasts of future exchange rates are probably even less accurate.

Suppose the company did have a forecasting model for exchange rates that outperformed the International Fisher Effect. It could then obtain unlimited wealth for its owners by using the model to exploit interest rate arbitrage opportunities, as explained in Chapter 8. If the company doesn't have enough confidence in its exchange rate forecasts to engage in interest rate arbitrage (very few companies engage in interest rate arbitrage), it should probably rely on this simple approach to capital budgeting.

Nevertheless, readers are advised to be familiar with the reasons and assumptions underlying this simplified approach. Most companies continue to incorporate specific exchange rate forecasts into their capital budgeting analyses.

ADJUSTED PRESENT VALUE

Our discussion of the Net Present Value technique for making capital budgeting decisions has focused on exchange rates and time value, ignoring the difficulties of estimating expected future foreign currency cash flows. The company must adjust these expected cash flows, along with its required rates of return, for the effects of political risks such as taxation and restrictions on remittances.

When these adjustments are large or particularly complex, the use of a special form of Net Present Value estimate, called adjusted present value, may be useful. Although the adjusted present value technique is complex in practice and beyond the scope of this book, the reader can benefit by being familiar with the essential characteristics of this approach to capital budgeting.

The principle behind *adjusted present value* is quite simple. The company breaks each period's net cash flow into separate risk categories. For each risk category, it computes the present value of the cash flows for every period, using a discount rate for that risk category. The present values of the separate risk categories are then added and the company's outlay for the project is subtracted to yield the adjusted present value for the project. Like Net Present Value, adjusted present value constitutes an estimate of the net value of the project to the company.

For example, suppose an American business is considering an investment in Mexico. There is little uncertainty about the subsidiary's future expenses, but the revenues in pesos are very uncertain. Taxes are also uncertain along with the ability to repatriate principal on a concessionary loan. The first step is to aggregate the cash flows according to their risk class. Second, an appropriate risk class is determined for each category, and the present dollar value is calculated. The separate present values are then summed and the present value of the investment outlay subtracted. If the result is positive, the investment is accepted.

CHAPTER PERSPECTIVE

Direct foreign investment is more complicated and risky than foreign investment in financial assets. Nevertheless, multinational corporations are playing a growing role in the world and national economies. Motives behind this growth include political, economic, and competitive factors. Multinationals are often able to exploit tax benefits, resources, and markets that are simply unavailable to purely domestic corporations.

The evaluation of direct foreign investment is based upon the Net Present Value concept. This is complicated by the need to forecast future currency exchange rates. The relationship between exchange rate changes and relative interest rates embodied in the International Fisher Effect can be used to simplify the analysis. In situations where the future benefits of direct foreign investment can be categorized into risk classes, a variant of Net Present Value, called adjusted present value analysis, can be useful.

International Banking

INTRODUCTION AND MAIN POINTS
Banks are among the most multinational of all companies. They pursue international operations in attempts to diversify their lending, seek out new depositors, and avoid regulations. Because both investors and business managers need to deal with multinational banks, they can benefit from an understanding of the basic structure and functions of multinational banks.

This chapter begins by exploring the nature of the explosive growth in Eurobanks and the Eurocurrency markets that they have created. Next, the different types of multinational banking organizations are explained. The chapter concludes with a discussion of regulation and a description of the world's central banking organizations.

After studying the material in this chapter:
- You will understand the nature and causes of growth in Eurobanking.
- You will understand the operation of the Eurocurrency market.
- You will be able to distinguish the different types of multinational banking organizations and be familiar with the services that they can provide.
- You will understand the organization and function of the International Monetary Fund and the World Bank.

EUROBANKS AND THE EUROCURRENCY MARKETS
Eurocurrencies are bank deposits that are denominated in currencies other than the currency of the nation in which the bank is located. Dollar deposits in London and Frankfurt are Eurodollars. Deutsche mark deposits in London and New York are Euromarks. Although dollar deposits in Tokyo and Singapore are sometimes called Asiadollars, these too are now often referred to as Eurodollars.

Eurobanks are banks that accept Eurocurrency deposits and use these funds to make Eurocurrency loans. Eurobanks are often subsidiaries or branches of major multinational banks. Virtually all large multinational banks engage in Eurobanking.

Banks are attracted to Eurobanking activities by the relative absence of regulations and the enormous size of the Eurocurrency market. Because Eurobanks deal in foreign currency, they are usually exempt from reserve requirements and deposit insurance regulations such as capital adequacy requirements and the payment of deposit insurance premiums.

Although many countries would like to regulate the Eurocurrency market, they find themselves caught in a form of competitive deregulation. Any nation that attempts to impose regulations, reserve requirements, or insurance premiums on the Eurocurrency market quickly experiences a flight of Eurobanks from its borders. In an age of efficient communications and fund transfers, Eurobanks can operate from and transfer operations to any one of dozens of countries.

In the United States, regulators have watched the worldwide dominance of the American banking industry erode to the point where it now plays a relatively minor role in international capital markets. American regulators have been forced to deregulate Eurocurrency activities in an attempt to reverse the competitive disadvantage and halt the erosion. Absent the U.S. government's role as the world's largest borrower, this erosion would have been more rapid.

The growth of the Eurocurrency market to the point where it now overshadows the United States banking system is even more remarkable in light of the fact that the Eurocurrency markets did not exist prior to World War II. The Eurocurrency markets began after the war when Communist countries that held dollars refused to deposit them in American banks and chose to deposit their dollars in and make transactions through London banks. These British banks earned interest on these deposits by making the first Eurodollar loans.

For years, the Eurodollar market remained small. However, in the 1960s, the U.S. government attempted to regulate lower interest rates in America with the Interest Equalization Tax and Regulation Q. American and European multinational corporations and banks found that they could avoid these by using the Eurodollar market.

The trend accelerated in the 1970s when the Organization of Petroleum Exporting Countries (OPEC) was accumulating massive dollar deposits from oil sales. OPEC deposited them in European banks in order to earn higher rates of return and avoid potential interference by the U.S. government. This practice continued through the 1980s.

Today, the Eurocurrency markets continue to grow as the result of efficiencies derived from economies of scale and the absence of reserve requirements and other regulations. Although the Eurodollar continues to dominate the Eurocurrency market, Euromarkets for other currencies, particularly the deutsche mark, are growing rapidly.

A more recent but popular development are deposits and loans denominated in Special Drawing Rights (SDRs) and European Currency Units (ECUs). Euroloans are primarily short-term, as are Eurodeposits. However, Euroloans of much longer maturity are now commonplace. Most long-term Euroloans feature floating rates that are tied to the London Interbank Offer Rate (LIBOR).

MULTINATIONAL BANKING ORGANIZATIONS

In the U.S., a wide variety of regulations have been adopted to restrict concentration and promote competition in banking. Some of these regulations are now being relaxed as awareness of the declining status of U.S. banks increases. Nevertheless, a wide variety of organizational structures have evolved as a means of enabling U.S. banks to compete with foreign banks. Investors, bankers, and business managers need to be familiar with these basic structures if they are to benefit the most from international banking services. The following sections describe the most important structural forms.

Correspondent Banks

Correspondent banking arose in the U.S. as a result of prohibitions on interstate banking. In order to serve large national companies, banks developed arrangements with banks in other states in order to facilitate the provision of interstate banking services. Many small- and medium-sized banks make use of this same type of arrangement by having overseas correspondent banks. In countries that restrict entry or operations by foreign banks, even large multinational banks provide services via correspondent relationships.

A correspondent bank can facilitate the collection and transfer of funds or their transfer and disbursement in a foreign country. Correspondent banks can also participate in the syndication of loans and provide credit reporting services. Correspondents can be compensated in the form of mutual services, direct fees, or the maintenance of low- or no-interest correspondent deposits. Correspondent relationships, which can be formal and contractual or informal, enable banks to provide services to their customers in a variety of countries without the necessity of maintaining any overseas personnel.

Affiliate Banks

A *banking affiliate* is similar in function to a correspondent. However, an affiliate is partially owned by a foreign bank and is incorporated in the country in which it is located. Ownership and management are primarily local, but the ownership interest of the foreign bank provides a more formal relationship.

Affiliates are not controlled by the foreign bank. The equity position of the foreign bank is similar to a deposit maintained by a foreign correspondent in compensation for services. Sometimes the foreign bank provides expertise and services to the affiliate, and the equity relationship enables the foreign bank to share in the rewards that this brings to the affiliate. However, affiliates often compete against the foreign part-owner.

Consortiums and Syndicates

Consortium banks are special forms of affiliates. Consortium banks are partially owned by several foreign banks; local ownership is nonexistent or has only a small minority of the shares. No one foreign bank controls a majority of the shares. Consortium banks are often located in tax havens or in London.

Consortium banks often facilitate the organization of *multinational banking syndicates* formed to share a large loan or underwriting of securities. They enable banks to diversify their portfolios better and to avoid too much credit exposure to any one customer.

Subsidiary Banks

Subsidiary banks are locally incorporated but are either wholly owned or controlled by majority ownership of a foreign bank. Although controlled by a foreign bank, subsidiaries are subject to the banking regulations of only the country in which they are located. Some subsidiaries, particularly London subsidiaries of American banks, operate as multinational banks in the Eurocurrency market.

Subsidiary banks may offer some tax advantages to their foreign owners. However, the primary advantage is the avoidance of foreign banking regulations. Subsidiaries often arise out of the purchase of an operating domestic bank by a foreign bank.

Edge Act Corporations

U.S. banks are prohibited from direct ownership of foreign subsidiaries and affiliates. Equity positions can be taken by *Edge Act corporations*, which are special bank subsidiaries that are federally chartered and allowed to purchase equity in foreign companies. States can charter *agreement corporations* that enable Federal Reserve member banks to make investments in foreign banks after entering into an agreement with the Federal Reserve.

Edge Act corporations have also been used to avoid restrictions on interstate banking. An Edge Act corporation can open an office in another state in order to facilitate the provision of interstate banking services. Foreign banks that wish to operate in the U.S. can also set up Edge Act corporations. However, they are restricted to accepting deposits that are related to international commerce. Their lending practices are unrestricted.

International Banking Facilities

By the early 1980s, the size of the Eurodollar market exceeded the size of the domestic U.S. banking system. The government responded by permitting the creation of *international banking facilities* that enable banks to attract a portion of the Eurocurrency market to the U.S. International banking facilities are exempt from both reserve requirements and federal deposit insurance. U.S. international banking facilities are also exempt from federal and New York State income tax.

An international banking facility is not a separate corporation or subsidiary, but is more like a division or agency within the corporation. It maintains separate accounts for deposits and loans, but its profits and losses are reflected in the overall corporate income statement. In addition to U.S. banks, savings and loans, Edge Act corporations, and foreign financial institutions can set up international banking facilities.

International banking facilities have grown rapidly, although most of the growth has been in foreign-owned banks. There are now more than 500 in the U.S. Japan has now allowed the establishment of international banking facilities, and most of the growth in recent years has been in Japan.

U.S. regulatory authorities have placed a variety of restrictions on international banking facilities in order to avoid a loss of control over domestic monetary policy. While U.S. international banking facilities are unrestricted in dealing in the interbank Eurocurrency market, they cannot accept domestic deposits or make domestic loans and investments. Nonbank depositors are restricted to minimum transactions of $100,000 and a minimum maturity of two days.

Foreign Branches

Conceptually, the *foreign branch* is the simplest form of international banking. It is also the most common form for U.S. banks. A foreign branch has separate accounts for assets and liabilities but is legally part of the parent. Foreign branches can be defined as banks that have overseas owners and directors. When customers deal with a foreign branch, they are dealing directly with the parent bank, which is wholly responsible for the branch's activities.

Branch banks are subject to the laws and regulations of both the host country and the parent country. This includes reserve requirements, deposit insurance, and taxation. Hence, the most restrictive laws and regulations become binding. London has established itself as a leading international banking center, by *deregulating* most foreign branch bank activities.

Other countries have been forced to lessen their regulations in order to attract international banks to their shores. This has taken its most extreme form in the Caribbean and certain Asian countries, which have promoted the establishment of *shell branches*, that constitute little more than mail and communications facilities.

Resident Representatives and Banking Agencies

Sometimes banks wish to set up facilities to provide some services to their overseas customers but not a full range of banking services. *Resident representatives* are overseas offices that neither accept deposits nor make loans and investments. The resident representative office often coordinates the provision of these services from a local correspondent bank. Resident representatives do in some cases offer direct services, such as credit checks and assistance with local business customs and practices.

Bank agencies are much more like branch banks. They make loans, clear drafts and checks, and exchange currencies. Unlike branches they do not offer or accept deposits. This enables bank agencies to avoid many regulations associated with deposits, such as reserve requirements and deposit insurance. Because of the strictness of such regulations in the U.S., many foreign banks operate bank agencies in major U.S. cities.

CENTRAL BANK ACTIVITIES

Because sovereign nations are reluctant to accept the authority of a world central bank, international banking remains relatively unregulated. Efforts of individual countries to regulate international banking activity often serve only to drive activity offshore. There is a growing but as yet unsuccessful effort to adopt common reserve and deposit insurance requirements among the major free-market economic powers. In the forefront of this movement is the European Economic Community, which has made some progress in this area and seeks to do more.

For the less developed countries, a de facto world central banking system appears to be evolving under the leadership of the International Monetary Fund and the World Bank. Many of these countries have been forced to submit to this form of central banking authority as a consequence of their own failure to maintain liquidity and investor confidence. In the following sections we examine some of the attributes of this emerging world central banking system.

The International Monetary Fund

At the end of World War II, the allied powers met at Bretton Woods and agreed to establish the *International Monetary Fund* (IMF) (see Chapter 6). Until the early 1970s, the major focus of IMF lending was to assist countries in maintaining the value of their currencies. A country could borrow up to 450 percent of its quota and use the proceeds to purchase its currency in order to maintain value. In the 1960s, the IMF started issuing to members Special Drawing Rights (SDRs) that could also be used to purchase a country's currency. By the mid-1970s, the Bretton Woods agreement to maintain currency values had broken down, and the role of the IMF began to change.

The Jamaica Agreement of 1976 formally recognized the practice of floating exchange rates. The IMF sold most of its gold reserves but increased members' contributions and expanded the creation of SDRs. The increased funds enabled the IMF to provide loans to countries for the purpose of supporting the international financial system, which was pressured by the formation of the OPEC oil cartel and the resultant dramatic increase in the price of oil.

One of the most important agencies of the IMF is now its *Compensatory Financing Facility*, which lends primarily to less developed countries in order to help them service their external debt and stabilize the flow of imports and exports. The IMF uses its power as a lender to extract compliance with its own monetary and fiscal policy objectives from borrowers. In the same way, the IMF can influence the former members of the Soviet bloc that are currently seeking membership. The stronger Western economies have now increased their contributions to the IMF to over $180 billion as a means of inducing greater cooperation from less developed countries.

Development Banks

The Bretton Woods agreement also established the International Bank for Reconstruction and Development, which is commonly known as the *World Bank*. The World Bank was originally established to facilitate reconstruction of Europe's infrastructure after World War II. Now its primary function is very similar to and coordinated with that of the IMF. The World Bank often cooperates with other national development agencies and commercial banks in financing infrastructure and capital intensive projects in less developed countries and raises funds by issuing bonds in the private capital markets.

Two affiliates of the World Bank are also active in the economic development of poorer countries. The *International Development Association* provides subsidized, low interest, long-term loans to governments of poor countries. The *International Finance Corporation* participates in loans to and purchases of equity in private-sector businesses in less developed countries. Like the IMF, the World Bank frequently extracts monetary and other concessions from countries to which it lends.

In addition to the World Bank, a number of regional development banks are sponsored by groups of countries to facilitate multilateral subsidized lending to less developed countries. These include the *European Investment Bank*, which lends to member nations in Europe and Africa, and the *Inter-American Development Bank*, which lends to Latin America. There are also major regional development banks for Asia, Africa, and the Arab states.

EUROPEAN MONETARY UNION

The authority of international central banks is restricted to serving poorer countries that depend upon the funds that the central bank can funnel to them. An important exception to this is the emerging *European Monetary Union*.

After the collapse in the early 1970s of the Bretton Woods System for maintaining fixed exchange rates, the members of the Common Market and several other European countries began to float their currencies jointly against the dollar. This arrangement became known as the "snake." In 1978 the arrangement was formalized with the establishment of the European Monetary System, which pledged the members' assistance to each other in maintaining their relative currency values and created the *European Currency Unit* (ECU).

In 1982 the *European Monetary Cooperation Fund* (EMCF) was set up. The EMCF is responsible for issuing ECUs and for lending funds to member countries for the purpose of supporting their currency values. Members are required to contribute to both a short-term lending pool and a long-term lending pool. Although the European Monetary System is multilateral, Germany increasingly dominates policy, and the deutsche mark has emerged, along with the yen, as major reserve currencies and rivals to the dollar.

European currency integration is likely to proceed. The Single European Act of 1985 specifies the total integration of the European market for goods, services, labor, and capital by the end of 1992, necessitating the adoption of additional common regulatory requirements for financial institutions, especially with respect to reserve requirements and deposit insurance. *The Delors Report*, commissioned by the European Economic Community (EEC) in 1989, envisions the establishment of a system of European central banking along the lines of the U.S. Federal Reserve System and the emergence of a single currency.

CHAPTER PERSPECTIVE

Over the last two decades, banking has become a truly international business. Banks that restrict their activities to a single national market for either loans or deposits find themselves at a competitive disadvantage. This phenomenon is most readily apparent in the Eurocurrency markets, in which banks and their customers make loans and deposits in currencies other than the currency of the country in which the bank is located. Banks have evolved a wide variety of corporate structures that enable them to conduct business across national borders.

Attempts by national regulatory agencies to control or restrict activity in the international banking market have failed. This failure results from the ease with which international banks can transfer operations from one country to another, so that countries that wish to attract or retain banking within their borders must engage in a form of competitive deregulation.

The exceptions to deregulation of international banking are multilateral central banking activities. The IMF and the World Bank play an increasing role in the economic lives of poor developing countries. These countries endure interference in their sovereignty in order to gain access to the benefits of international capital markets. This desire to obtain benefits of international economic cooperation is also the driving force behind the integration of the European financial system. European monetary union may reflect factors that will serve to unify the world financial system in the future.

International Portfolio Management

INTRODUCTION AND MAIN POINTS

In the preceding chapters, we have viewed international capital markets primarily from the perspective of the corporation. In this chapter, we examine these markets from the investor's perspective. Although international stock markets are the major focus of this chapter, the investor's perspective on the international bond market is also included.

We begin by addressing diversification, which is the main economic motivation for international investment. Factors that inhibit international diversification, such as market structure, transaction costs, and taxation, are addressed. The chapter concludes by addressing the pros and cons of various techniques available for making international investments.

After studying the material in this chapter:

— You will understand the advantages and limitations of international diversification.

— You will be familiar with differences among countries in market structure and trading practices.

— You will understand the fundamental principles applied to the taxation of income from international investments.

— You will be familiar with various instruments designed to facilitate international investment, such as American Depository Receipts and international mutual funds.

RISK-RETURN CONCEPTS

During the 1950s and 1960s, world capital markets were dominated by the stock and bond markets in the U.S. In the 1990s, this is no longer true. Japanese stocks constitute almost 50 percent of the market value of all stocks traded in the world today, whereas American stocks constitute about 30 percent. British stocks constitute less than 10 percent, while German, Canadian, and French stocks each constitute about 2.5 percent. The next largest group are Swiss, Italian, and Australian stocks, which together constitute less than two percent of the total. The foreign share of stocks is growing much more rapidly than the U.S. share which constituted over half the world total as recently as 1984.

Foreign purchases of stocks in U.S. markets have been substantial for many years, recently totaling over half a trillion dollars per year. A more recent phenomenon is the increased purchase of foreign stocks by American investors. This behavior is understandable in light of the more rapid growth of foreign equity markets as compared to the American market. In the following sections, we analyze the motives behind these international investments.

Correlation Between International Stock Markets

Investors consider stocks risky in the sense that the rate of return on investment is highly variable. An investor can reduce this variability in return by investing in a portfolio of different stocks, as opposed to investing in only one stock, so that the losses on stocks that turn out to perform poorly are offset by gains on stocks that turn in a better than expected performance. Hence, portfolios provide the same average return as individual stocks but are less risky in the sense that the average return is less variable. This reduction in risk is called the *portfolio effect*.

The correlation between stock returns determines the amount of risk reduction that one can obtain from the portfolio effect. Highly correlated stocks experience similar changes in rates of return. A portfolio of highly correlated stocks provides an investor very little risk reduction, since when one stock returns less than expected, the other stocks tend to do the same. Hence, there are few unexpected gains to offset the losses. The reduction in risk associated with the portfolio effect is greatest when stocks exhibit the least correlation in returns.

Almost all stocks are correlated with each other to some extent. A stock's *systematic risk* is a measure of that portion of its risk that cannot be avoided by holding it in a portfolio of other stocks. Its *unsystematic risk* is the variability that can be avoided by holding it in a portfolio of other stocks. Hence, investors are unconcerned about a stock's risk, as long as it is unsystematic and they can therefore avoid it by holding a portfolio.

Foreign stocks can help investors reduce the risk of their portfolios to the extent that the foreign stock returns are uncorrelated with the returns on domestic stocks. Studies of returns on stocks listed in foreign exchanges confirm that they are only partially correlated with American stocks. The Dutch and Canadian stock markets are the most highly correlated with the U.S. market, yet less than one-third of their variability is related to variability in the U.S. market. Less than 10 percent of the variability in the Japanese market is related to variability in the U.S. market, and only about one-fourth to one-third of the variability in other nations' stock markets is related to the U.S. market.

There are several factors that cause stock market returns in different countries to be uncorrelated. A stock's return consists of both dividends paid and changes in price. For example an investor may purchase a stock for $20, receive $1 in dividends, and sell the stock after a year for $22. The investor's total rate of return is 15 percent, five percent in dividends plus 10 percent in capital gains.

In the long run, dividends and capital gains are determined by the company's earnings, which in turn depend upon technological, competitive, political, and economic factors. Political, competitive, and economic conditions in a particular country affect all business in that country; hence, all stock returns in a particular country are uncorrelated with stock returns in other countries. For example, environmental regulations, corporate income taxes, inflation rates, price controls, and the business cycle tend to affect all businesses in a particular country. Investors can hedge against the effects of these factors by investing in the stocks of many different countries.

Diversification Strategies

Diversification is an investment policy that reduces portfolio variability by exploiting the absence of perfect correlation in security returns. The simplest diversification strategy is the random selection of as many securities as possible. The problem with this strategy is that one must make a proportional investment in all securities in order to minimize variability in returns. Fortunately, investors pursuing this strategy can expect to obtain nearly 95 percent of all possible risk reduction by randomly selecting about 25 stocks. However, a random selection must include all possible stocks. If foreign stocks are excluded, the selection is not random, and the risk reduction will not be as great.

Another strategy is to measure the correlation of individual stocks and select a portfolio consisting of highly uncorrelated stocks. This strategy enables investors to achieve high levels of diversification with far fewer stocks. However, in practice it is often difficult to accurately measure the correlation of stocks.

Most estimates are based upon historic returns, which may or may not be accurate estimates of correlation in future returns.

Several studies indicate that the reduction in risk obtained from international diversification are enhanced by participation in the international bond market. Although there is disagreement as to the magnitude of the portfolio risk reduction, there is agreement that investors could have reduced the variability of their historic portfolio returns without sacrificing the average level of return by including a variety of international bonds.

Some studies have also explored the effect of hedging currency risk in internationally diversified portfolios. A portfolio manager can eliminate the variability in international returns caused by changes in exchange rates by hedging in the forward or futures currency markets.

Fluctuations in currency values may add variability to portfolio returns without increasing the average return obtained. Hence, portfolios that feature international investments in stocks and bonds but that are hedged in the forward or futures currency markets historically offer the lowest levels of risk for given levels of return.

COMPLICATING FACTORS

Although the hedging strategies described in the previous section are practiced by a few investors, international diversification in stocks and bonds along with hedging in the forward and futures currency markets has not been common practice. However, international investment grew very rapidly in the 1980s; in the U.S. the dollar amount of stock purchased by foreigners increased over 800 percent. The increase was even more rapid in Japan and Germany.

Since investors are risk averse, it is likely that some factors may be inhibiting international diversification. The following sections describe some of these factors, along with the forces that are reducing their impact.

Restrictions on Foreign Investment

Evidence suggests that foreign stock and bond markets are segmented from each other. The causes are both direct and indirect. The direct causes of segmentation include legal barriers to foreign ownership of domestic stocks and regulations that restrict the flow of investment overseas. Indirect causes include political and social inspired boycotts.

For example, many countries restrict the allowable percent of foreign ownership of domestic companies. Mexico and India limit foreign equity control to 49 percent of the voting shares in any one company; France and Sweden limit foreign ownership to 20 percent of any one company. Many Eastern countries historically prohibited any foreign ownership of businesses. In the U.S., legislation has been introduced, but not adopted, to limit foreign control of domestic companies.

Another form of direct regulation restricting international diversification is the control of investment capital flowing overseas. Many less developed countries prohibit any overseas investment by their nationals. Even industrialized countries have introduced restrictions. For example, Britain and France have in the past required investors to exchange currency at unfavorable rates if the funds were to be used for overseas investment. During the 1960s, the U.S. government imposed interest equalization taxes in order to reduce the appeal of high rates of return on investments in Europe.

Sometimes governments or political groups prohibit investment in particular countries. For example, several states, unions, and universities have prohibited their pension funds from investing in South African companies. In addition, some Arab governments have attempted to restrict investment in companies that do business with Israel.

Market Structure

Differences in the organization of markets and the methods of trading securities can also inhibit foreign investment. There are three basic market structures for trading securities. Private stock exchanges, such as those in the U.S., are independent although regulated corporations. The members own the stock of the corporation and are free within the limits of any government regulations to adopt trading procedures and commissions as they see fit. Their rules are primarily constrained by competition from other exchanges.

Public bourses such as the Paris Bourse are established and owned by the government to facilitate securities trading. Public bourses are government monopolies, and membership is governed by public appointments. Regulations and fees are determined by the government. In recent years, growing international competition has started to force public bourses to deregulate.

In some countries, such as Germany, both stock and bond trading is controlled by the banks. Sometimes large nonbank financial institutions, such as insurers and pension funds, participate. Government regulations are imposed on either the banks or the exchange.

Securities markets also differ according to whether they are based on cash or forward transactions. Forward markets for stocks are prohibited in Germany and Japan, whereas Britain, France, and many less developed countries rely on forward markets. In the U.S., most trading is done in cash markets, but forward markets exist for many indices and derivative securities.

Forward markets clear all transactions at specific time intervals. For example, all trades on the Paris Bourse are cleared monthly, which eliminates many offsetting transactions. This practice also provides investors with considerable leverage, since only a deposit is required prior to actually clearing the trade. Leverage can also be provided in cash markets where margin trading is allowed.

Security prices can be determined by either continuous quotation or by auction at specific intervals. Continuous quotes require specialists or dealers in a security to offer to buy or to sell securities at quoted prices. The difference between the selling price (ask price) and the buying price (bid price) provides a profit to the specialist or dealer and constitutes an additional cost to the investor.

Auction pricing takes place at specific times during the trading day. There are two commonly used types of auction. An *order matching system* is suitable for low-volume markets. In this system, all orders to buy specify a maximum price and all orders to sell specify a minimum price. These orders are accumulated over a period of time, and a clerk or in some cases a computer, periodically compares the buy and sell orders and selects a price at which the maximum number of trades will take place. All trades are then made at this price. Buy and sell orders are then accumulated for the next period.

The *call auction system* is used in most large stock exchanges. In a call auction, the auctioneer calls out a price and traders indicate how many shares they want to buy or sell. If the buy orders exceed the sell orders, the auctioneer calls out a higher price. If the sell orders exceed the buy orders, the auctioneer calls out a lower price. No trading takes place until the auctioneer calls out a price at which the traders wish to buy and sell the same number of shares. Even in continuous markets such as the U.S. and Japan, specialists use a form of call auction to determine opening prices at the start of the session.

Transaction Costs

Transaction costs of trading in foreign markets include the bid/ask spread, the broker's commission, and information costs.

Bid/ask spreads occur only in continuous markets; their magnitude is controlled by competition among specialists and by exchange rules on pricing increments.

Commissions vary widely in different markets and countries. Commissions are negotiated and, hence, controlled by competition in the U.S., whereas most commissions overseas are regulated by either the exchange or the host government, although there is a trend toward negotiated commissions. The "Big Bang" is a reference to the deregulation of the London financial markets in 1986, an important part of which was the adoption of negotiated commissions. In order to avoid competitive disadvantages vis-à-vis London, other European exchanges are being forced to move in the same direction.

The costs of obtaining information about foreign stocks and trading practices constitute another transaction cost. Often investors must pay for translation services in addition to the costs of locating and transmitting the information in a timely fashion. As the volume of international trading increases and the technological facilities for international communication improve, these costs will continue to fall rapidly.

Taxation

Taxation frequently constitutes a major impediment to international diversification. Investors have to contend with both foreign and domestic government taxation, although some countries have tax treaties that prevent or reduce double taxation. Other countries allow investors to deduct or, in some cases, credit foreign taxes paid when computing their tax. Taxation can be applied both to income in the form of interest or dividends and to capital gains, either when realized or when accrued. Outside of the U.S., many countries do not tax capital gains; other countries adjust capital gains for inflation and avoid taxing artificial gains on inflated stock values.

Outside the U.S., some countries collect transaction taxes when securities are bought and/or sold. In the U.S., these taxes can be collected by state or municipal governments; however, fear of exchange relocation to other localities keeps these transaction taxes low.

INVESTING IN FOREIGN SECURITIES

Market segmentation, taxation, and transaction and information costs all serve to inhibit the pursuit of the benefits of international diversification. A variety of alternatives are available to investors who seek the benefits of international diversification without incurring these costs. The following sections present some of the more commonly used methods.

Multinational Corporations

The simplest way to obtain the benefits of international diversification without incurring the costs is to invest in the stocks of domestic corporations that do a substantial portion of their business overseas. This strategy is motivated by the idea that economic fluctuations in various countries tend to be uncorrelated. Economic prosperity in one country provides profits to offset losses in countries with depressed economies.

Unfortunately, a wide variety of studies have shown that historically this approach has failed to provide much diversification. Furthermore, the growing integration of the world economy suggests that the results of this strategy will not improve in the future. The surprising absence of diversification benefits from investing in multinationals is generally attributed to the means by which investors discount or price future expected earnings. A company's earnings are discounted according to required rates of return on similar assets. Apparently investors' multinational stocks are priced in relation to domestic rather than to worldwide rates of return.

Dual Listings

Some large multinationals list company shares for sale in several countries. The motives are varied. Some companies are simply too large with respect to their domestic markets to find enough investors in one country. Others list in several countries in order to gain access to perceived differences in required rates of return in segmented markets resulting from trading practices, transaction costs, and tax policies.

The problem with dual listing is cost. Exchanges charge substantial fees for listing and require compliance with a variety of regulations concerning securities characteristics and disclosure of financial data. These costs are often added to by government regulations that are applied to foreign and domestic or, in some cases, only foreign companies.

Several studies of historic performance seem to indicate that the cost of dual listing outweighs the benefits. Only a limited number of companies in countries with large, well-developed domestic capital markets pursue this route.

American Depository Receipts

One recent innovation that has demonstrated an ability to provide American investors substantial international diversification is the *American Depository Receipt* (ADR). U.S. banks create ADRs by purchasing large amounts of a foreign company's stock overseas and depositing the stock in a trust account. The bank then sells shares of ownership (ADRs) in the trust to investors.

These ADRs may be equal in number to the number of shares of stock in the trust, in which case one ADR corresponds to ownership of one share of stock. Usually, there are fewer ADRs than shares of stock, so each ADR typically represents ownership of multiple shares of foreign stock. When the foreign company pays a dividend, the bank converts it to dollars at the current exchange rate and distributes it proportionately to the owners of the ADRs.

There is almost always a well-developed secondary market for ADRs. Nearly 100 of the more popular ADRs are listed on the New York Stock Exchange. However, the majority are traded in the over-the-counter market. Some foreign companies sponsor their own ADRs, paying all the fees associated with listing and finding a sponsoring bank. In many cases banks create ADRs independently of the foreign company.

Although ADRs are priced in dollars and trade independently of the foreign stock, which trades in its own currency value, the value of ADRs is closely related to the value of the foreign stock. If the price of an ADR differs from the dollar value of the foreign stock when converted at the current exchange rate, arbitrageurs can make a profit. If the ADR is selling for less, the arbitrageurs sell the foreign stock. After converting the proceeds from the foreign stock sale to dollars, they have more than enough dollars to buy the ADRs. The difference is their profit. This drives up the price of the ADR and reduces the price of the foreign stock until they are equal and there is no more arbitrage profit. Hence, arbitrage serves to maintain equality between the dollar value of the ADR and the underlying stock.

ADRs appear to provide many of the benefits of international diversification to investors, while avoiding many of the costs. Banks charge fees for creating and maintaining ADRs. Some very large investors may find it cheaper to make their foreign security purchases directly.

International Mutual Funds

Smaller investors seeking an alternative to ADRs can purchase shares in mutual funds that include foreign stocks in their portfolios.

Mutual funds are either open- or closed-end. *Open-end mutual funds* sell shares and use the proceeds to buy and sell other securities on a continuing basis. The mutual fund shareholder owns a percentage of whatever is in the portfolio.

A *closed-end mutual fund* is more like an ADR that represents a trust in which are deposited the shares of many different companies. While the number of shares in an open-end mutual fund can vary, the number of shares in a closed-end fund is fixed.

Mutual funds are not without cost to the investor. Both charge a periodic fee for servicing the fund. In addition, many also charge a sales commission for purchasing and/or selling shares of the fund. These fees vary widely among different funds.

Some funds provide global diversification and are passively managed. Others specialize in specific countries, regions, and/or investment objectives. Some funds emphasize growth and incur substantial risks, while others emphasize income and avoid as much risk as possible. Some even pursue active strategies to hedge exchange rate risk.

CHAPTER PERSPECTIVE

Widespread studies leave little doubt that internationally diversified investment portfolios subject investors to less risk for a given level of return than do purely domestic portfolios. Since investors are risk averse, they can benefit from international investment. Unfortunately, the benefits of international diversification are often offset by costs related to market segmentation, taxation, regulation, communication, information, and trading. Nevertheless, the benefits outweigh the costs for very large investors.

In recent years a number of innovations in the securities markets have evolved that enable smaller investors to take advantage of international diversification. Primary among these are American Depository Receipts and international mutual funds. Although these instruments are not without their own costs, the benefits of international diversification appear to outweigh them.

Glossary

Accounting exposure variability in the firm's reported values for net income and net worth that results from changes in exchange rates.

Accounts payable a balance sheet liability entry that reflects the amount of funds owed by the firm to its suppliers for goods and services already received.

Accounts receivable a balance sheet asset entry that reflects the amount of funds owed to the firm by its customers. Accounts payable arise when the firm delivers goods and services and allows for later payment.

Adjusted present value a method for computing the net present value of a project that features cash flows with different risk characteristics. The different types of cash flows can be estimated and discounted separately.

Agencies special offices set up by some multinational banks that can make loans but are not able to accept deposits.

Agreement corporations subsidiaries of banks that are allowed to offer international banking services across borders.

American Depository Receipt special securities issued by banks that reflect ownership of a portion of a foreign company's stock that is held in trust by the bank. American Depository Receipts trade for a dollar price that reflects the effects of both the foreign stock's performance and the exchange rate.

American terms a method of exchange rate quotation that gives the value of a foreign currency in U.S. dollars.

Appreciation an increase in the value of one currency in terms of another currency. When the dollar appreciates, it can be exchanged for greater amounts of foreign currencies.

Arbitrageur an individual or institution who profits by buying and selling the same item or items that are economically equivalent.

Asiacurrencies a bank deposit in an Asian country that is denominated in the currency of another country. A U.S. dollar deposit in a bank in Singapore is an Asiadollar.

Ask price the price that a dealer is asking customers to pay for a currency. It is also known as the *offer rate*.

Back to back loan when firms in two countries wish to borrow each other's currency, they can make an offsetting arrangement to pay off each other's loan at maturity. This eliminates their exposure to exchange rate changes. When such an arrangement is negotiated by a bank, it is known as *link financing*.

Balance of payments a national accounting statement that records the size of all cash inflows and outflows from a country over a period of time. Balance of payments reflects imports, exports, foreign borrowing, lending, investments along with international transfers, and payments by governments.

Balance of trade the value of a country's exports minus that country's imports.

Balance sheet an accounting report that shows the historic cost less depreciation of all of a firm's assets along with the book value of all the firm's liabilities and equity accounts.

Bank draft an order to pay some institution or individual funds drawn from a particular account at a bank. Drafts differ from checks in that they do not have to be signed by the owner of the account from which they are drawn. Also called a *bill of exchange*.

Banker's acceptance a bank time draft that has been discounted prior to maturity and sold in the secondary money market after being guaranteed by the issuing bank.

Bank for International Settlements an international banking facility located in Switzerland that promotes cooperation among central banks and serves as the lender of last resort to some less developed countries.

Barter a system of trade in which exchanges of goods and/or services are arranged. It avoids exchange rate risk, since no currencies are involved.

Bearer bonds unregistered bonds that are negotiable and feature coupons attached to the bond. Investors in bearer bonds are difficult to trace and identify. This anonymity attracts some investors.

Beta a statistical measure of a security's nondiversifiable risk. Securities with higher betas feature higher returns to compensate for the risk.

Bid-ask spread the amount by which the ask rate exceeds the bid rate for a currency. Dealers must charge more for a currency than they are willing to pay or they will go out of business.

Bid price the price that a dealer is willing to pay for a particular currency.

Big Bang the deregulation of London securities markets in 1986. Foreign firms were allowed entry and commisions were set by competition.

Bill of exchange an order to pay some institution or individual funds drawn from a particular account at a bank. Bills of exchange differ from checks in that they do not have to be signed by the owner of the account from which they are drawn. They are also called *bank drafts*.

Bill of lading a shipping receipt for goods in transit. A bill of lading can also constitute title to the goods in some cases.

Black market refers to the means by which those who want to sell currency at prices higher than the legal price can transact currencies with those who are willing to pay more than the legal price. In the absence of government regulation, a black market becomes a free market.

Black market rate the price at which the supply equals the demand for a currency on the black market.

Blocked currency a currency that a particular government prevents from being converted in the foreign exchange market. Governments that are trying to keep the value of their currency up sometimes block its supply to the foreign exchange market.

Branch a fully functional office of a multinational bank. Branches can offer any banking service allowed by local regulations.

Bretton Woods Agreement an international agreement by the Western powers at the end of World War II to maintain a system of fixed exchange rates by establishing the price of the dollar in gold and the prices of all other currencies in terms of the dollar.

Bulldog bonds pound denominated bonds sold in Britain by foreign firms.

Call option the right to buy a specified asset at a specified price within a specified amount of time. Currency call options exist both for specific amounts of currency and for currency futures contracts.

Capital long-term funds available for investment. Sometimes capital refers only to equity funds, but more often to equity and long-term debt.

Capital budgeting the process for determining the firm's long-term investment in fixed assets such as plant, equipment, and property.

Capital market the market for long-term funds such as stocks and bonds. It is contrasted with the *money market*, which is the market for short-term funds.

Central bank a government institution in each country that is responsible for controlling the money supply and the nation's banking system. In the United States the Federal Reserve is the central bank.

CHIPS (Clearing House Interbank Payment System) an electronic system for transferring funds between banks.

Clearinghouse an institutional arrangement that facilitates the receipt and payment of funds. All of an institution's receipts and payments for a day are accrued at the clearinghouse. Most receipts are offset by payments. Only the difference requires an actual funds transfer.

Common Market an economic arrangement between the Western European nations that facilitates trade by lowering regulatory and tariff barriers. It is also called the *European Economic Community* (EEC).

Comparative advantage the economic motive and determinant of international trade. Countries increase their economic prosperity by exporting the goods that they are relatively more efficient at producing and importing the goods that other countries are relatively more efficient at producing.

Concession agreement a contract between a host country's government and a foreign firm that wants to invest in the host country. Concession agreements are usually negotiated prior to investment and spell out such things as taxes, remittance of profits, and transfer of ownership.

Consignment the shipment of goods to a foreign country prior to the transfer of title to the goods.

Consular invoice a shipping document that is required for exporting certain goods to certain countries. Before some countries will allow some goods to enter their country, they require the certification of the goods by their commercial consul in the exporting country.

Convertible currency a currency for which there are no barriers or restrictions in the foreign exchange market.

Correlation a statistical measure of the degree of relatedness between two variables. Perfect positive correlation means a percentage increase in one variable is matched by the same increase in the other variable. Perfect negative correlation means an increase in one corresponds to a decrease in the other.

Correspondent bank a bank that provides banking services for another bank in a different location or country in return for deposits or fees.

Cost of capital the rate of return that investors require in return for supplying funds to the firm.

Counterpurchase a method of trading goods and services internationally that avoids the use and subsequent exchange of currencies. Unlike *barter*, counterpurchase does not specify which goods will be exchanged, only the total values of the goods to be exchanged.

Countertrade any arrangement for exchanging goods and services without exchanging currency. *Barter* and *counterpurchase* are forms of countertrade.

Country fund a mutual fund that invests its funds only in the stock of a particular foreign country. Country funds are usually closed-end.

Covenants restrictions on the activity of the firm that are spelled out in the bond indenture. Covenants protect the interests of the bondholders from actions by management on behalf of stockholders.

Covered interest arbitrage the process of borrowing funds in one country and converting them into another country's currency where they are lent. Covered means that the risk of converting the funds back into the original currency to pay off the loan at maturity is eliminated by purchasing that currency in the forward market.

Credit risk the risk that the importer of goods shipped by a foreign firm on credit will default.

Cross hedging hedging transaction exposure in one currency by contracting in another currency that is highly correlated. Cross hedging is only practiced when hedging contracts are unavailable for the currency to which the firm is exposed.

Cross listing the practice of simultaneously listing a firm's stock on exchanges in several different countries at the same time.

Cross rate the effective exchange rate between two currencies that can be obtained by exchanging each currency for a third currency.

Cumulative translation adjustment account a special balance sheet item listed under the firms equity accounts in accordance with FASB 52. It enables a multinational firm to adjust its assets and liabilities to reflect current exchange rates without booking changes in net worth on the firm's income statement.

Currency cocktails bonds or loans for which the principal and interest are denominated in a weighted average of several currencies.

Currency swap an exchange of currencies between two firms that is reversed at a specific rate and time in the future.

Current account a national balance of payments account that includes international trade in goods and services along with transfer payments and short-term credit.

Current rate method an accounting procedure for translating financial statements from one currency into another at the current exchange rate.

Delphi technique a subjective means for evaluating the political risk associated with a particular country. It consists primarily of the opinions of experts in foreign affairs.

Depreciation a reduction in the value of a fixed asset due to age and use. Accounting depreciation is based upon mathematical rules. Economic depreciation reflects loss of economic value.

Devaluation a reduction in the value of one currency in terms of another currency. When the dollar depreciates, it can be exchanged for fewer units of foreign currency.

Direct quote the value of a foreign currency in units of the domestic currency. A direct quote on the pound in America would be a dollar value, whereas a direct quote for the value of the pound in Germany would be a deutsche mark value.

Dirty float a system in which exchange rates are determined by supply and demand in the foreign exchange market, but where goverments buy and sell currencies in order to influence the market.

DISC (Domestic International Sales Corporations) specially chartered firms that obtain tax advantages in return for promoting U.S. exports.

Discounting using accounts receivable as collateral in order to obtain short-term loans.

Diversification the reduction in the variability of an average return on several investments that occurs when the individual returns are not perfectly positively correlated.

Dual currency bonds bonds for which the principal will be paid in either of two currencies. Investors can choose the most advatageous currency at maturity.

████████ the sale of goods in a foreign country at a price below the cost of production to the exporting firm. This strategy is pursued to gain market share or in some cases to export unemployment during recessions.

Economic efficiency the allocation of resources to their highest valued use and the production and distribution of goods and services at the lowest possible cost. The unfettered pursuit of self-interest in a perfectly competitive economy leads to economic efficiency.

Economic exposure variations in the economic or market value of the firm that result from changes in exchange rates. This is due primarily to changes in the firm's competitiveness with importers and exporters.

Economies of scale reductions in the average cost of producing goods and services that result from producing larger quantities.

ECU (European Currency Unit) a weighted average of the currencies of common market countries. The weights reflect the relative size of the national economies.

Edge Act Corporation subsidiaries of U.S. banks that are allowed to offer international banking services across state and national borders.

Efficient market a market in which prices accurately reflect all available information. Arbitrageurs cannot make profits in efficient markets.

Eurobanking banking that involves accepting deposits and making loans that are denominated in many different currencies besides the host country's currency.

Eurobond bonds that are denominated in the currency of countries other than the currency of the country in which they are sold.

Eurocommercial paper short-term notes that are issued by firms and denominated in currencies of countries other than the one in which they are sold.

Eurodollars dollar denominated deposits in banks located outside the United States. Most Eurodollars are deposited in London. Dollar deposits in International Banking Facilities in the United States are also Eurodollars.

Euronote intermediate term notes denominated in the currency of a country other than the currency of the country in which they are sold.

European Economic Community (EEC) an economic arrangement between the Western European nations that facilitates trade by lowering regulatory and tariff barriers. It is also called the *common market*.

European Monetary System (EMS) an agreement of common market countries, excluding Britain, to maintain a fixed set of exchange rates among members' currencies.

European terms a method of exchange rate quotation whereby the value of the dollar is given in units of foreign currency, such as francs per dollar or lire per dollar.

Ex ante return the expected return on an investment.

Exchange rate the ratio of exchange between two currencies. Also, the market price of a currency in terms of another currency.

Exercise price the price that one must pay for an asset that is bought or sold with an option contract. It is also called the *striking* or *strike price*.

Export the sale and delivery of goods and services to a customer in a foreign country.

Export Import Bank a U.S. government agency that facilitates international trade. Its primary activity is providing low cost financing for imports and exports.

Ex post return the actual return earned on an investment.

Exposure netting a procedure used by multinational firms to reduce the costs of hedging transaction exposure. It relies on the principal of netting inflows and outflows of currencies.

Expropriation the involuntary seizure by a host government of foreign owned businesses and other assets without adequate compensation.

Factor the sale of securities and accounts receivables at a reduced price prior to maturity.

FASB 52 the accounting method currently approved by the Financial Accounting Standards Board for use in translating financial statements from one currency to another.

Fiat money currency that is made legal tender by government law or regulation. In the United States, Federal Reserve Notes are fiat money. Fiat money always has a legal value that exceeds its intrinsic value.

FIFO (First In First Out) an accounting procedure governing how the cost of goods sold from inventory are determined. FIFO increases reported earnings by costing out lower cost inventory against revenues.

Fiscal policy government economic policy with respect to taxation and expenditures. A stimulative fiscal policy would be to increase the budget deficit by reducing taxes or increasing spending.

Fisher effect an economic relation between interest rates and inflation rates. Interest rates reflect expected inflation rates.

Fixed exchange rate an exchange rate that doesn't vary. Governments fix exchange rates by buying and selling currencies in the foreign exchange market.

Floating exchange rate an exchange rate that varies according to the economic factors that influence supply and demand for currencies. Floating exchange rates are determined by market forces.

Floating rate note a debt security that features an interest rate that varies over the life of the loan in accordance with changes in market interest rates.

Foreign bond a bond issued by a foreign company in the domestic bond market. Unlike Eurobonds, foreign bonds sold in the United States are denominated in dollars.

Foreign tax credit a reduction in domestic taxes that is equal to the amount of foreign taxes paid on the same income.

Forfaiting a method of financing the purchase of capital goods by East Bloc countries. The forfaiter coordinates the activities of exporters, importers, and financial institutions.

Forward contract a contract to purchase a specified amount of currency at specified price at a specified time in the future.

Forward discount the percentage by which the forward rate is below the spot rate.

Forward premium the percentage by which the forward rate exceeds the spot rate.

Forward rate the exchange rate or price of a currency specified in a forward contract.

Fronting loan a loan by a multinational corporation to a foreign affiliate that is funneled through a multinational bank.

FSC (Foreign Sales Corporation) a type of firm engaged in exports that provides tax exempt income to its investors.

Functional currency the primary currency in which a foreign subsidiary conducts its business. FASB 52 specifies the rules for determining a functional currency.

Futures contract a standardized and guaranteed forward contract. The contracts are standardized with respect to price, quantity, and maturity. The standardization and guarantee makes possible the trading of futures contracts prior to maturity.

GATT (General Agreement on Tariffs and Trade) an international agreement to encourage trade by the reduction of tariffs and quotas on foreign goods and services.

Global Fisher Effect an economic equilibrium that exhibits an equality of expected real interest rates amoung countries when there are no restrictions on international trade, credit, and currency exchanges.

Gold standard an international exchange rate equilibrium that results when all governments permit the exchange of their currencies for gold. If the gold price of currencies is fixed, then exchange rates are fixed.

Gold tranche the portion of a country's IMF reserve that is pledged in gold. A country may borrow its gold tranche without obtaining permission.

Group of Seven the major Western economic powers: Britain, Canada, France, Germany, Italy, Japan, and the United States. They meet periodically to coordinate global monetary policy.

Hedging any procedure that eliminates or reduces variability in future cash flows. If future dollar cash flows form investments that are uncertain due to uncertainty about future exchange rates, then additional investments can be made that offer dollar payouts that are inversely related. The net dollar cash flow from the two investments is less variable.

Hyperinflation an extremely high rate of inflation that destroys the value of and confidence in a currency.

IBRD (International Bank for Reconstruction and Development) an international banking organization that is owned by member countries of the IMF and makes loans that promote economic development. It is more commonly referred to as the World Bank.

IMM (International Monetary Market) a division of the Chicago Mercantile Exchange that is responsible for currency futures and options.

Imports the purchase and receipt of foreign-made goods and services into a country.

Indexed bonds bonds that feature principal repayments that are tied either to the price level or the exchange rate. Some indexed bonds also feature interest payments that are tied to price levels or exchange rates.

Indirect quote a method of quoting an exchange rate that gives the number of foreign currency units per unit of domestic currency. An indirect quote for the yen in America would be the number of yen per dollar.

Informational efficiency the degree to which market prices accurately reflect the value of all information about an asset.

Interbank market the means by which banks buy and sell assets to and from each other. Transaction costs and spreads on currencies, deposits, and loans are the lowest in the interbank market.

Interest equalization tax a tax that is imposed on interest and earnings from foreign investments that serves to equate returns on foreign investment with returns on domestic investment.

Interest rate parity an equilibrium relationship between spot and forward exchange rates and foreign and domestic interest rates. Banks use interest rate parity to price forward exchange.

Interest rate swap an exchange of either interest receipts or interest expenses between two firms. For example, one firm may wish to avoid locking in a fixed long-term interest rate, whereas another wishes to avoid the uncertainty of a variable short-term interest rate. They can swap their positions.

International banking facility special departments of U.S. banks that are free to accept dollar deposits and make loans to foreign residents without reserve requirements or interest rate regulations. They are permitted so that U.S. banks can pursue business in the Eurodollar market.

IRR (Internal Rate of Return) the rate of return at which the present value of cash invested is equal to the present value of the cash earned.

Joint venture a firm that is owned and controlled by more than one independent firm. Foreign firms often engaged in joint ventures with a domestic firm, sharing expertise in different areas of the business.

Kangaroo bonds bonds denominated in Australian dollars and sold in Australia by foreign firms.

Lagging delaying payment or receipt of a foreign currency until there is an offsetting transaction for the purpose of reducing transaction exposure.

Law of one price an equilibrium between the price of a tradable good in one country and its price in another country. Arbitrage ensures that the prices are equivalent when translated at the current exchange rate.

LDC (Less Developed Country) a term used to describe countries in a poor and more primitive economic condition.

Leading accelerating payment or receipt of a foreign currency until there is an offsetting transaction for the purpose of reducing transaction exposure.

Letter of credit a contractual commitment by a bank to make payment for goods shipped to an importer. This eliminates the exposure of exporters to credit risk.

LIBOR (London Interbank Offer Rate) an interbank market interest rate in Eurocurrency deposits lent by banks to one another. Many loans have interest rates tied to LIBOR.

Licensing a procedure whereby a foreign firm permits a domestic firm to produce and market goods on its behalf in return for royalties on sales or a share of profits.

LIFFE (London International Financial Futures Exchange) a British-based clearinghouse that offers financial futures and options. It is a rapidly growing competitor of U.S. based exchanges.

LIFO (Last In First Out) an accounting procedure governing how the cost of goods sold from inventory are determined. LIFO decreases reported earnings and taxes by costing out higher cost inventory against revenues.

Link financing a financing technique where banks arrange for two firms in two countries to borrow each other's currency and then make an offsetting arrangement to pay off each other's loan at maturity. This eliminates their exposure to exchange rate changes.

Liquidity the degree to which an asset can be converted into currency without delay and without loss of value.

Locational arbitrage the simultaneous buying and selling of a currency in two different locations. Profit is made by buying at a low price and selling at a high price. This serves to drive the prices to equality.

Ltd. (Limited) a British term for a corporation.

Managed float a description of a government policy that allows market forces to determine a currency's exchange rate but does not rule out government efforts to influence these market forces.

Market efficiency the degree to which market-determined prices accurately reflect the true economic value of assets.

Market value the price at which the supply of an asset equals the demand for the asset.

Monetary/nonmonetary method an accounting procedure for translating accounting statements from one currency to another. This method specifies that monetary assets and liabilities be translated at current exhange rates, whereas nonmonetary assets and liabilities be translated at historic exhange rates.

Monetary policy the efforts of a nation's central bank aimed at influencing inflation rates, economic growth, and interest rates by varying the supply of money.

Money market the markets for short-term financial assets such as t-bills, commercial paper, and banker's acceptances.

Money market hedge elimination or reduction of a firm's transaction exposure by simultaneously borrowing in one currency and lending in another currency.

Most favored nation a designation by the U.S. government that lowers tariffs and other restrictions on imports from that nation. It also permits assistance from the Export Import Bank.

Multilateral netting a method of reducing transaction exposure that offsets receipts in one currency with payments in other currencies that have values that are highly correlated with it.

Mutual fund an investment company that sells shares in order to raise funds for the purpose of investing in other securities, such as stocks and bonds. Mutual funds may sell a limited number of shares (closed-end) or an unlimited number of shares (open-end).

Negotiable security a security that can be sold prior to maturity to another investor in the secondary market. Examples include stocks, bonds, t-bills, commercial paper, and banker's acceptances.

Net present value the present value of cash inflows minus the present value of cash outflows.

Netting a procedure used by multinational firms to reduce the costs of hedging transaction exposure. It relies on the principle of netting inflows and outflows of currencies.

NIFs (Note Issuance Facilities) an arrangement where a group of banks buys the short-term debt of firms and resells it in the Eurocurrency markets.

Nominal rate the rate of return on an investment that is unadjusted for the effect of inflation. It is distinguished from the real rate, which is the nominal rate less the rate of inflation.

OECD (Organization for Economic Cooperation and Development) a group of the major Western economic powers that cooperates to improve international economic development.

Offer rate the price at which a foreign exchange dealer will sell a foreign currency. It is also called the *asking price*.

Official exchange rate the legal price of a regulated currency as distinguished from the black market price.

Official reserves deposits of gold, currency, and SDRs held at the IMF by member countries.

Offsetting trade a form of countertrade in which a country agrees to import an amount of goods and services in order to export an amount of goods and services.

Offshore exchange rate the market price of a regulated currency outside the legal jurisdiction of the regulating government. It is similar to a legal black market rate.

Open account the sale of goods and services on credit up to a specified maximum amount.

Open market operations the purchase and sale of financial assets (primarily t-bills) by the government for the purpose of controlling the money supply. The purchase of a t-bill increases the money supply and lowers interest rates, whereas the sale of t-bills reduces the money supply and raises interest rates.

Operating exposure the degree to which a change in the exchange rate influences a firm's future revenues and expenses.

OPIC (Overseas Private Investment Corporation) a corporation sponsored by the U.S. government that insures firms' foreign investments against exposure to political risk.

Option the right (not an obligation) to buy or sell an asset at a specified price (exercise price) within a specified period of time.

Parallel loan an arrangement by which two independent firms with separate foreign subsidiaries in their respective countries make offsetting loans to each other's subsidiaries. This procedure makes the companies indifferent to exhange rate changes.

Payments netting a procedure used by multinational firms to reduce the costs of hedging transaction exposure. It relies on the principle of netting inflows and outflows of currencies.

PEFCO (Private Export Funding Corporation) a corporation established by the U.S. government to facilitate unsubsidized funding of U.S. exports.

Pegged exchange rate under Bretton Woods, governments maintained (pegged) the dollar value of all currencies within one percent. A similar procedure is used in the European Monetary System.

Petrodollars dollar revenues of oil producing nations that are deposited with banks in the Eurodollar market.

Planned divestment a part of a concession agreement in which the foreign investor agrees to gradually sell its equity in its subsidiary to the host government or private investors in the host country.

Points one percent of an asset's price. Points are used to describe the changes in an asset's selling price. Sometimes points can refer to one one-hundreth of a percent.

Political risk variability in the value of a foreign investment that is caused by political factors ranging from tax rate changes to expropriation.

Pooling the transfer of cash balances from a multinational's subsidiaries around the world to a centralized cash management facility.

Portfolio a collection of different kinds of financial assets. Portfolios enable investors to diversify some of their investment risks.

Portfolio risk the amount of variability in the average return on a portfolio.

Protectionism a government policy that restricts imports for the purpose of allowing less competitive domestic firms to raise prices to consumers and increase profits and employment.

Purchasing power a measure of the amount of goods and services that an individual can obtain for a specified amount of income.

Purchasing power parity an equilibrium condition in which changes in exhange rates reflect changes in the underlying values of currencies as a result of different inflation rates.

Put option a contract that gives the owner the right to sell a specified amount of currency at a specified exchange rate within a specified amount of time.

Quota a limit on the amount of goods and services that can be imported or exported. Quotas can be enforced by governments or agreed to voluntarily in order to prevent economic disruptions.

Quote a listed price at which a currency can be bought and sold.

Rational expectations an economic theory that states that asset prices reflect to best informed expectations of future values. Market efficiency is a form of rational expectations theory.

Real exchange rate the value of an exchange rate after adjusting for the effect of inflation on the underlying value of the two currencies.

Real interest rate the rate of return on an asset after adjustment to eliminate the effect of inflation.

Recourse a contractual provision inserted into the financing sales contract for some assets that specifies the seller is obligated to repurchase the asset in the event that the buyer defaults on the loan.

Registered bond a bond whose owner is recorded by the issuer or trustee for the bond. This makes it difficult to steal the bond, but also difficult to conceal the identity of the owner.

Rembrandt bond a bond denominated in guilders and sold in the Netherlands by foreign firms.

Remittance the payment of profits, royalties, and management fees by a foreign subsidiary to the parent firm.

Reporting currency the currency of the parent firm into which a foreign subsidiary's financial statements must be translated under *FASB 52*.

Revaluation an increase in the foreign currency value of a currency.

RUF (Revolving Underwriting Facility) an arrangement where a group of banks buy the short-term debt of firms and resell it in the Eurocurrency markets.

SA (Sociedad Anonima or Societe Anonyme) the respective Spanish and French designations for a corporation.

Samurai bonds a yen denominated bond that is sold in Japan by a foreign firm.

SARL (Societa a Responsabilita Limitada) the Italian designation for a firm with limited liability.

SDR (Special Drawing Right) a special type of reserves used by central banks and issued by the International Monetary Fund. Its value is a weighted average of the dollar, deutsche mark, pound, franc, and yen.

Sensitivity analysis a form of risk analysis that shows the effect on financial variables of changes in factors whose future economic value is uncertain.

Shoguns any bond that is sold in Japan but denominated in a currency other than the yen.

Short sale the sale of a financial asset that one does not own. The purpose is to profit from a future reduction in the asset's price, since the "borrowed" asset can be replaced in the future at a lower price.

SIBOR (Singapore Interbank Offer Rate) the rate at which Asiadollar deposits are lent by banks to each other. It has similar uses to *LIBOR*.

Sight draft a bill of exchange that is honored by the bank immediately.

SIMEX (Singapore International Monetary Exchange) a futures exchange and clearinghouse based in Singapore that competes with the IMM and LIFFE.

Simulation a projection of future outcomes based upon assumed values for unknown economic variables.

Smithsonian Agreement an attempt in the early 1970s to prevent the collapse of the Bretton Woods system of fixed exchange rates. There were two Smithsonian Agreements, but both failed to prevent the collapse. which was complete by 1974.

Snake a system developed by the EEC countries (with the exception of Britain) for maintaining fixed exchange rates with respect to the deutsche mark, while allowing the deutsche mark to float against other currencies such as the dollar.

SNIF (Standby Note Issuance Facility) an arrangement where a group of banks buy the short-term debt of firms and resell it in the Eurocurrency markets.

Sovereign risk variablity in the value of a foreign firm or investment that results from uncertainty about future government action. It is also called *political* or *country risk.*

SPA (Societa per Azioni) the Italian designation for a corporation.

Speculation a high-risk investment strategy that is based upon the investor's belief that an asset can be purchased for significantly less than it is worth or sold for significantly more than it is worth.

Spot rate the price at which a currency can be purchased or sold and then delivered within two business days.

Striking price the price that is paid or received for an asset when an option contract is exercised. It is also known as the exercise price or strike price.

Stripped bonds investment bankers purchase bonds and then sell the coupon interest payments and principal payment separately. They are also called strips.

Subsidiary a firm that is incorporated in one country but wholly owned by a firm in another country.

Sunk costs expenditures that cannot be recovered even if a project is terminated and the assets sold.

Sushi bonds a yen denominated bond that is sold in Japan by a foreign firm.

Swap rate the difference between the forward exchange rate on a currency and its spot exchange rate.

SWIFT (Society for Worldwide Interbank Financial Telecommunications) an interbank telecommunications network for confirming international funds transfers.

Syndicate a group of investors (usually commercial or investment banks) that participate jointly in purchasing and selling assets (generally financial assets).

Systematic risk that portion of the variability in future returns on an investment that cannot be diversified away. Investors require a risk premium for bearing this kind of risk.

Tariff a tax on imported goods and services. It is also called a duty.

Tax haven a nation where the laws concerning taxation and income accounting permit a foreign firm to lower its taxes on income produced elsewhere.

Temporal method a method for translating financial statements into another currency that was embodied in FASB 8.

Terms of trade a measure of the extent of economic benefits that a country obtains by participating in international trade.

Time draft a bill of exchange that will be honored by a bank at maturity. Time drafts can be discounted, if funds are needed immediately.

Trade acceptance a time draft that is guaranted by a nonbank firm and sold in the secondary money market. It is similar to a banker's acceptance but more risky.

Transaction exposure variablity in the domestic currency value of a known future receipt of foreign currency.

Transfer pricing the price that a subsidiary charges another subsidiary of the same firm for goods and services supplied to it. Manipulation of transfer prices can be used to move profits from a high tax country to a low tax country.

Translation converting accounting or economic values in one currency into another currency.

Translation exposure changes in reported net income and net worth that are caused by changes in exchange rates used to translate accounting statements in foreign currencies.

Triangular arbitrage the simultaneous purchase and sale of a currency at its cross rate and direct exchange rate in order to make a profit.

Unbiased forecast a forecast that is on average neither too high nor too low.

Unbiased forward rate a forward exchange rate that is neither greater than nor less than the best informed expectation of the future spot exchange rate.

Unbundling breaking a remittance from a foreign subsidiary to its parent firm into separate parts. Firms practice unbundling in order to deal with restrictions imposed on remittances in foreign countries.

Unlevered financed without the use of debt.

Unsystematic risk variability in the future returns on an investment that can be diversified away by holding a portfolio of randomly selected investments. Investors do not require a risk premium for bearing unsystematic risk.

Usance the maturity of a time draft. It is also called the tenor.

Value added tax (VAT) a method of taxation widely used in Europe that imposes a tax on goods and services at each stage of production and delivery equal to the value added to the product at that stage. It is similar to a national sales tax.

World Bank an international financial institution that is sponsored by members of the IMF for the purpose of lending funds to less developed countries in order to promote economic growth. More formally it is called the International Bank for Reconstruction and Development.

Yankee bond a bond that is denominated in dollars and sold in the United States by foreign firms.

Y.K. (Yugen-Kaisha) Japanese designation for a corporation.

Zero coupon bond a bond that pays no coupon interest. Because they sell at a deep discount, they appreciate as they approach maturity, when they pay their face value.

Index

J. Manville Harris, Jr., is an associate professor of finance at Clemson University. Previously, he was an assistant professor of finance at Virginia Tech and the University of Georgia. He received his Ph.D. in finance from the University of South Carolina. He has taught undergraduate, M.B.A., and Ph.D. level courses in international finance and corporate finance over the past twelve years. He has published both research and tutorial articles in a wide variety of journals, including the *Journal of Finance*, the *Journal of Financial Education,* the *Journal of Financial Research,* and the *Journal of Business Research.* His research has been reported on in several finance textbooks and *USA Today.*